LEGAL ISSUES IN SPORT AND PHYSICAL EDUCATION MANAGEMENT

JOHN N. DROWATZKY, J.D., Ed.D.

Professor of Exercise Science and Physical Education
The University of Toledo

ISBN 0-87563-426-5

Published by
STIPES PUBLISHING COMPANY
10–12 Chester Street
Champaign, Illinois 61820

It is a professional pr————————— Monographs in Sport and Physical Education as an i——————————' Physical Education and Recreation list. This new sei——————————asis to keep pace with the continuing expansion of spe——————————ysical education, and also because the term "sport" is——————————ierica and throughout the entire world. Management——————————it the term "managerial revolution" is well understo——————————eveloping profession based on an ever more sophisticat—————

We are projecting a s——————————graphs. These paperbacks will provide basic, useful m——————————iture, in the area of sport and physical education mana————————————————a variety of ways, and they will be relatively inexpensive in this period of burgeoning book prices.

A considerable range of topics is possible for inclusion in this exploratory series ranging from legal matters to marketing to change process to inventory control—to what have you? We have outstanding people in mind to develop these monographs in the best possible way.

We are grateful to the late R. A. Stipes, Jr., for his support over several decades. This ongoing relationship with him and Bob Watts could not have been better. We trust that this new series will provide solid, useful material for the future.

Earle F. Zeigler
Series Editor

TABLE OF CONTENTS

CHAPTER 1

INTRODUCTION

We live in a society governed by a legal system that produced a living, changing body of laws. These changes can occur either through legislative enactment of new laws or by the body of common law produced by court decisions that become the precedence for future decisions. The past few years have seen legal changes making a significant impact on the conduct of sport and physical education programs. These changes in the legal system increased the complexity of instructional, coaching and administrative jobs associated with these fields of endeavor. This monograph will highlight legal issues important in the management of sport and physical education and make recommendations for dealing with these issues.

In the legal world each situation is analyzed independently to see how it is both similar to and different from past court decisions. Consequently, any current situation will receive the same kind of individual scrutiny, but some generalizations can be made about what will be viewed as appropriate professional conduct. These generalizations will be used to form the guidelines provided in this monograph. Before dealing with legal issues, a brief look at the impact of recent professional changes that have legal implications is worthwhile.

Two of the major legal requirements that have resulted in an increased impact for professionals in sport and physical education are accountability and responsibility. A brief look at factors that produced the increased demands for better accountability and responsibility will help in understanding the guidelines presented in the remainder of this monograph. These factors do not operate in isolation, but interact with one another, producing an impact greater than if only one were present.

> MAJOR LEGAL ISSUES IN SPORT
> Accountability
> Fiscal Responsibility
> Legislative Requirements

The first factor increasing accountability and responsibility is that of finances. This is due to a couple of reasons: first, financial support is necessary if any program is to be successful; and, second, financial support is a major concern at all levels of administration and professional endeavor. One thing about sport participation is certain: the costs have risen dramatically. This increase is due to many things: inflationary effects on travel, salary, equipment and facilities; more participants because of increased programs for girls and women and handicapped persons; a greater number of activities; and increased emphasis on safety. Second, the increased number of activities and participants also requires that more coaches, officials and other personnel must be hired. At the same time programmatic costs have increased, public support for educational and extracurricular activities has decreased.

Third, there has been a simultaneous demand for more fiscal accountability which, in turn, produced higher administrative overhead. This increased accountability results from several features. Among these features are: 1) the larger number of people being served; 2) increased people and financial resources required to conduct the programs; 3) changes in the public and other funding of such programs; and 4) political pressures and the politicians' response to these pressures.

A fourth factor compounding all of the administrative and coaching jobs is the increased knowledge possessed by the public and athletes. Today, many athletes *already* have years of coaching and competition by the time they enter high school programs. This situation is particularly evident in athletes who have participated in age group swimming, club tennis, little league baseball and softball, pee wee football, community soccer, and age group gymnastics programs. The presence of such experienced and highly skilled athletes in programs places entirely different demands upon physical educators and coaches in the public schools. The schools are pressured to provide more teams and activities, while at the same time public financial support for extracurricular programs is declining. Women and handicapped persons must have equality of opportunity for physical education and athletic experience. Teaching and coaching personnel having the knowledge and experience to handle students possessing a greater variety of background and ability are required.

Fifth, athletic equipment has changed dramatically; today we have oversized tennis racquets, fiberglass pole vaulting poles, isokinetic weight training, durable football helmets with little tolerance in fitting, and artificial turf to name but a few examples. Many products are touted as ergogenic aids, and many sports applications have been developed for television and computers. Many students are willing to use performance enhancing drugs to improve their chances to win, to obtain scholarships and/or improve their appearance.

Sixth, spectators are an important source of funds for many athletic programs. Further, spectators are often more knowledgeable about sports because of expert commentary and the instant replay accompanying television sport programs. Officials are challenged more and more. The spectators must have safe facilities from which to watch and administrators are responsible for crowd control and aspects of spectator safety.

The final factor producing increased accountability and responsibility for sport and physical education professionals is the increased involvement of the legal system. Politicians at all levels have passed laws that have an impact upon programs. Two such examples are Title IX for Women and Education for All Handicapped Children Act of 1975. Legal requirements such as due process have been extended to education and extracurricular activities. The legal concept of product liability has evolved and people are more ready to sue for presumed liability or negligence. The earlier mentioned increases in strength, size, skill and knowledge possessed by performers has had a great influence on the responsibilities imposed by courts.

This brief summary of influences producing increased accountability and responsibility for sport and physical education professionals leads to the first recommendations of this monograph. These recommendations are:

1. *Have Adequate Planning.* Planning is necessary to make sure that your instruction and coaching is well organized, involves the proper equipment, uses appropriate techniques, covers the pertinent technique, skill and safety factors and follows a logical progression. Be sure your unit, lesson and coaching plans are written, followed and kept on file. Plan for accidents and emergencies. Likewise, keep copies of accident reports, permissions and other pertinent documents.

2. *Update Your Education.* Keep abreast of new developments and techniques in conditioning, skills instruction, safety aspects, equipment changes, first aid, athletic training and others associated with your profession. Regular attendance at classes, seminars, workshops and other professional opportunities for continuing education can make a difference. Likewise, read professional journals and attend professional meetings to improve your skill and knowledge.

3. *Maintain Communications*. It is so important to have good communication for many reasons. However, perhaps the two most important are associated with the legal requirement of notice and due process procedures, and the prevention of isolation from students, athletes and parents. In the legal context, one cannot be held responsible for following rules and regulations or be subject to discipline without prior notice (communication) about such rules and regulations. In a practical context, people are much more likely to sue professionals who are isolated and distant. For these reasons alone, communication is important.

4. *Think of Safety First*. Get in the habit of planning for safety whenever you make other plans. If you are going to build a new building, make safety plans for crowd management, participation and other functions designed and/or intended for the building or its parts a design factor. Make periodic, regular safety inspections a part of your regular maintenance plans. Include safety instruction when developing lesson, unit and coaching plans. In a word, become safety conscious!

CHAPTER 2

NEGLIGENCE

The past few years have been accompanied by many changes impacting professionals in sport and physical education. While these changes were briefly mentioned in the introductory chapter, it is important to reemphasize the present high level of participation in sports activity by the public. This increased participation, both in numbers of participants and activities offered, increases the need for adequate sports instruction. Further, accompanying increased sports instruction and participation is an increased probability that the professional will need to deal with injuries. The public has also become more aware of legal rights and the number of lawsuits filed against instructors, coaches and administrators has increased. It is, of course, impossible to prevent injuries, as they are an inevitable part of physical activity and sports participation. The legal system imposes a duty on coaches, teachers and other professionals to prevent unreasonable risk of harm to students and participants. The question is, therefore, how much foresight, care, supervision and instruction must be provided to meet the professional's duty. The legal name of the failure to meet this duty is negligence.

THE PROFESSIONAL'S DUTY

Once the injured participant or those persons responsible for the injured party believe that the injury suffered is related to the professional's negligence, the situation is taken into court for resolution. A goal of all professionals is to prevent situations which provide the basis for legal action from occurring. To accomplish this end, an understanding of the duties involved in teaching and coaching must be considered. Duties are imposed upon professionals from several sources, federal and/or state constitutions, legislation, and the common law that evolved through precedents established in cases decided by the various courts. Of these three, common law is usually more important in resolving liability or negligence issues resulting from injuries during participation.

> DUTY: To use due care to prevent unreasonable risk of harm to others.

When resolving the situation, the courts dealing with torts, the legal term defining this issue, looks for the presence of four elements. These elements are:

A Duty. In the case of sport and physical education professionals, the duty is to use due care to prevent an unreasonable risk of harm.

A Breach of This Duty. This is the situation in which the professional does not meet the standard of care, usually either through inappropriate actions or a failure to act.

An Injury. The plaintiff participant must have an injury, either physical or mental. Damages are assessed for this injury by the jury or judge.

Proximate Cause. This concept means that the injury must have been caused by the professional's breach of duty. The attorneys often call this the "but for" test; would the injury have occurred but for this breach of duty.

If it can be shown that the injury was caused by a breach of the duty to protect others from unreasonable physical or mental harm, and to avoid acts or omissions that might produce such harm, then the professional becomes liable. Such libellous conduct is called negligent conduct; that is, conduct that falls below a standard of care established by law to protect others from an unreasonable risk of harm.

Torts (Second) presents the standards used for conduct and a professional undertaking as follows.

Section 284. Negligent Conduct; Act or Failure to Act.

Negligent conduct may be either:

(a) An act which the actor as a reasonable man should recognize as involving an unreasonable risk of causing an invasion of an interest of another, or

(b) A failure to do an act which is necessary for the protection or assistance of another and which the actor is under a duty to do.

Section 299 A. Undertaking in Profession or Trade.

Unless he represents that he has greater or less skill or knowledge, one who undertakes to render services in the practice of a profession or trade is required to exercise the skill and knowledge normally possessed by members of that profession or trade in good standing in similar communities.

In the practical situation, the determination of liability and one's duty will depend upon all the facts and circumstances surrounding the injury. The courts usually weigh the following factors presented by Terry (1915).

1. The value of that which is exposed to the risk; in our case, students are given the highest value in the formula.

2. The reason for the conduct of the person taking the risk. For example, did the student perform the activity knowingly and voluntarily with an understanding of all possible consequences or did the student act because the instructor said to perform?

3. The magnitude of the risk; is the potential injury a bruised ego or broken bones?

4. The utility of the risk.

5. The necessity of the risk; is there some other activity which would produce the same result without the risk?

Vacca (1974) characterized teacher negligence as flowing from the failure to carry out a duty owed a student, an unreasonable performance for a duty owed the student and/or dereliction in the safety and upkeep of all supplies and equipment used by students. Although parents of injured children may not hesitate to bring legal action against a teacher, the courts do not appear to place an unreasonable burden of care upon coaches and physical educators. Proehl (1959, p. 753) noted that . . .

> Few laymen profess ignorance of the mysteries of teaching; indeed in no field of endeavor are the professionals subjected to so much non-professional advice and interference. And the area of discretion is small: methods of teaching and

of maintaining classroom discipline have been so standardized and regulated that the teacher who departs from the standard is as likely to find himself censured by his principal or his board as by a truculent parent.

Examination of cases involving teacher's liability for negligence reveal . . . that in the common law jurisdiction there is a reluctance to find negligence in actions against teachers even in situations where the status of teacher qua teacher has fundamentally nothing to do with the question of liability. . . .

Langerman and Fidel (1977) presented guidelines for trial lawyers to follow in sports injury cases. They suggested several areas where duties were commonly breached by teachers or coaches. Among the areas suggested that trial lawyers scrutinize for negligence are: 1) safety in equipment and facilities; 2) use of progressive instructional and coaching methods; 3) matching opponents with like abilities; 4) providing instruction in safety procedures; and 5) past injury check-up procedures. Other legal experts point to coaches and teachers having a careless or indifferent attitude toward the safety and interests of others and failure to use common sense in approaching situations as prime reasons for negligent conduct. Consequently, lawyers have identified these specific areas of sport and physical education instruction as generally producing negligence on the part of teachers and coaches and they begin their search for a breach of duty correspondingly.

Following a review of cases involving injuries in athletic and physical education activities, Drowatzky (1977) proposed several guidelines that teachers and coaches should follow during the conduct of their activities to minimize the potential for litigation from injuries suffered during their coaching or teaching. The following guidelines are based on this research and an example of how courts applied their analyses are presented as suggestions to follow during instruction or coaching physical activities. Each problem area is presented individually and several guidelines have been developed.

AREAS OF NEGLIGENCE
Instruction
Supervision
Student Attributes
Equipment

INSTRUCTION

The courts look at several aspects of instruction when determining whether the instructor fulfilled the duty imposed by common law or statutory law. The following guidelines emphasize the major responsibilities that are present during instruction or coaching.

1. *Instruction is a duty that cannot be delegated.*

Most states have legislation that makes the teacher or coach employed by the school district or university responsible for the instruction given to the students. Duties are also established by the contract signed by the faculty member and these contracts make instruction a responsibility of the teacher. Courts generally rule that teaching contracts include the teacher's promise to render professional services and perform such other services as are reasonably related to the teacher's professional preparation and welfare of the school (Hazard, 1978).

Further, the body of common law established by courts over the years recognizes this principle. In Bellman v. San Francisco High School District, testimony indicated that the physical education teacher gave the student no direct instruction, but allowed advanced students in the class to show the plaintiff how to do the gymnastic exercise (the "roll over two") that produced the injury. Subsequently, the court found that the class teacher did not properly instruct and supervise the student in accord with the teacher's responsibility for proper instruction. (Also see Gardner v. State cited in guideline 5.)

The instructor must, therefore, either present the instruction directly, or in the case of a student teacher or teacher's aide, supervise the instruction that is presented to the students following the standards established in the local jurisdiction. Responsible instruction presented or closely supervised by the instructor or coach is a must. Under no circumstances should the task of instruction be delegated to other students.

2. *Adequate instruction must include the skills and techniques necessary for proper performance.*

> The participant must receive instruction in the skills and techniques necessary for proper performance as well as the rules of the game. Often in the rush to make physical activities interesting and active, instructors or coaches will give students superficial practice on the individual skills and techniques used in the game. The professional is often more concerned about the potential for boredom during drills than the development of skill necessary for safe and efficient participation.

The court in Vendrell v. School District addressed the issue of adequate instruction in determining whether the coach was negligent when one of his football players became a permanent paraplegic following a neck injury. The neck injury resulted when the player charged head first into approaching tacklers in an attempt to gain extra distance. The coach and school district were found not guilty of negligence because of the following facts presented in the case. All potential team members were given a physical exam by a physician and the injured player was determined to be physically fit. The athletes were put through an extensive training program that included calisthenics, instruction in physical conditioning and training, instruction in the fundamental skills required in the game, and how to use protective equipment to absorb blows. The coach had stressed proper fundamentals as an essential aspect of both successful play and self-protection. The court was impressed by the instruction and conditioning used to prepare the athletes for the shocks, blows and other rough treatment that would be present in actual play. This case provides a good example of how to prevent negligence.

3. *Instruction must include reasonable safety precautions.*

> In some situations coaches and instructors do a sufficient job in providing instruction in skills and strategy, but omit instruction that relates to safety. This omission may take any of several forms: failure to use spotters, failure to instruct spotters before using them, failure to alert participants to potential dangers in the activity, or failure to teach participants how to react to dangerous situations that arise during participation.

An example of the last situation arose when a 10-year-old boy was injured from a collision with another boy while playing line soccer during soccer class. While doing a good job of teaching soccer skills, the facts indicated that the coach did not tell the class what a player should do if two players met the ball at the same time. As a consequence, the court (in Darrow v. West Genesee Central School District) held that reasonable care requires a demonstration and explanation of the game, and what two players should do when they meet the ball at the same time. Schools have an affirmative duty to instruct students in physical education classes and sport programs on reasonable safety precautions that are to be observed. Based on this decision, it follows that teachers and coaches should be alert to potential dangers and how the participants should react for safety, as well as the skill, technique and strategy aspects of the game.

4. *Instruction must be presented clearly and unambiguously.*

When the teacher or coach gives directions or instructions, they must be presented in such a manner that the students will not misunderstand and the directions must make the correct manner of performance clear. If the students can perform the task in more than one way and still be within the confines of the instructions, then the instructions do not possess sufficient clarity.

For example, the teacher involved in the case of Armlin v. Board of Education was found negligent in the instructions issued to 5th grade students performing on the rings. This teacher told the students they could do anything they wanted on the rings except swing, and to get out of the rings by going backwards so they would come down on their feet. No demonstrations were provided and spotters were not instructed as to how to perform. One student suffered severe back injuries when while performing on the rings she stood in the rings and jumped out backwards, an act clearly within the instructions provided by the teacher. The critical feature noted in this case was the absence of clear, appropriate instruction. It is important to give instruction that is not ambiguous and is at a level which can be understood by the students.

5. *Adequate instruction requires the use of customary teaching methods and a logical progression of materials.*

Failure of the teacher to instruct the child using the customary method of instruction was found to be the proximate cause of the child's injury in Gardner v. State. According to the facts presented, an 11-year-old student was injured while attempting a headstand during a physical education class. The specific omissions during instruction included a failure to give adequate strengthening and preparatory activities before attempting to teach the headstand. Further, the specific instruction provided during the time at which the injury occurred was provided by a student teacher who was in the third year of the teacher preparation curriculum. This situation was also contrary to the first principle in this section, namely that instruction cannot be delegated. Thus, absence of these factors indicated that adequate instruction was not present in this situation.

If instructors deviate from approved courses of study or an approved, official syllabus, they do so at their own risk and must be capable of showing that their plan was an equally approved method of instruction. The teacher in Keesee v. Board of Education was faced with a common problem, a large class, and decided to depart from the syllabus to provide more opportunity for activity for the students. She modified the activity and had eight relatively inexperienced junior high school girls contending for the possession of the ball during a game of line soccer. The syllabus indicated that only two girls should be actively chasing the ball during the game. The syllabus also indicated that the girls should begin from a standing position rather than on the run as was the teacher's practice. During the game, several of the girls fell on the plaintiff, causing the injury. The court also noticed that there was little, if any, skills instruction, as the teacher claimed that the students could acquire all the necessary skill through participation in one session of line soccer. Needless to say, this teacher was held liable for the injury. The court concluded that such practice was a disregard for the safety and welfare of the students, regardless of her motivation to enable more girls to participate in the game.

As these two cases have indicated, instruction must follow a logical progression and be presented according to an approved instructional method. The best way to prove that such was the case, if the need should arise, is by providing unit plans and lesson plans. The unit plans should show the instructional progression, and the lesson plans should show specifically what material was included in the lesson and that the instruction conformed to accepted educational practices. Take the time to do a good job of preparation and then keep the materials on file for future use. If you discover problems, correct them on your plans and incorporate them into the next set of lesson plans. While lesson and unit plans are directed toward the teachers, coaches should follow the same practices when developing their practice plans. Well-developed plans would help show that adequate instructions, preparation and coaching techniques were used if the need should arise.

6. *Adequate instruction includes presentation of the unique characteristics of equipment and teaching its proper use.*

As will be discussed later in product liability, dangerous equipment, such as the modern football helmet, requires special instructions. It is the manufacturer's duty to provide these instructions, but it is the coach's duty to make sure that the team members receive and understand these instructions. Any time the teacher or coach uses equipment that is either dangerous or unique, he or she must discuss the characteristics and safety procedures associated with the equipment. Other common examples would include the trampoline, springboards in diving and gymnastics, protective equipment used in baseball or softball, and eye protection required in racquetball and similar sports. Such presentations should become a standard part of the instructions that are given with the activity.

The lawsuit in Grant v. Lake Oswego School District arose from injuries received by students bounding on a springboard and hitting their heads on a doorway. The students were directed to place the springboard in a storeroom after class, which they did, but then one student began to bounce on it, striking his head on the doorway above the springboard. The court observed that the students had not received in-depth instructions regarding the springboard's use and its characteristics, particularly regarding the danger of its use in areas with low ceilings. Further, the teacher did not tell the students how to make it harmless in storage (by turning it on its side), nor did the teacher check to make sure it was stored in the prescribed manner. Thus, the teacher was found negligent in the area of instruction.

SUPERVISION

The teacher does not provide continual instruction, but is also supervising students during changing and passing periods and activity periods. Coaches have much the same type of supervisory responsibility. As a consequence, questions arise as to the type of duty associated with supervision during the different types of activities associated with sport and physical education: instruction or coaching; activity periods and practice; shower and changing periods; pre-class warmup; and passing periods between classes. Courts are in general agreement about these responsibilities.

The duty required during instruction is that of providing a reasonable amount of supervision necessary to prevent an unreasonable risk of harm to the students. Courts generally hold that *general* supervision is required in the gymnasium and locker areas during the changing of classes, but *direct, specific* supervision is required during the conduct of physical activity programs (Kerby v. Elk Grove Union High School District). Supervision thus imposes the duty of ordinary care, and this requires that one foresee the need for additional supervision should it arise. There is no hard and fast rule as the degree of supervision required will vary with the foreseeable danger or hazard present in the circumstances (see 38 ALR 3rd 830).

Since supervision imposes a duty to foresee that increased supervision may be needed, if the coach or teacher detects such a condition, they should tell the administration immediately and follow the verbal report up with a written letter or memo that begins "This letter is sent to confirm my report that a potentially dangerous condition . . ." followed by a restatement of the problem. Be sure to keep a carbon copy of the statement and, if no remedial action is taken, write another memo and ask what they wish you to do in the situation.

Courts have held that a variety of situations produce negligence in supervision. An overcrowded gymnasium with 48 students simultaneously playing 3-man basketball on 8 courts created a condition with unreasonable supervision (Bauer v. Board of Education). Likewise, one teacher supervising 20 to 25 students participating on 4 trampolines was not reasonable supervision (Chilton v. Cook County School District).

Teachers generally must be physically present, especially during physical activity classes to provide supervision. They must take characteristics of the students into account when determining reasonable supervision. The age and maturity level of the students are important factors and, if the age characteristics tend toward rowdyism and rough, dangerous practices, greater care is required during supervision (Tymkowicz v. San Jose Unified School District; Cirillo v. City of Milwaukee). Sports like golf, which are not likely to be perceived as dangerous by the students, require careful arrangement of the teaching stations and close supervision of the students during participation and instruction to prevent undue risk of injury (Brahatcek v. Millard School District).

Another factor determining the degree of supervision required is the dangerousness of the activity. If an activity has been declared inherently dangerous by a court, then a high standard of care is imposed by the court. In Carabba v. Anacortes School District, negligence was found during the supervision of an interscholastic wrestling match when an official had his attention diverted from the contestants for a few seconds during which time an injury occurred. If the activity is compulsory—that is, the instructor requires the students to perform the activity after they have told the instructor of their fear—then a higher standard of care is also imposed (Cherney v. Board of Education). The highest standard of care is applied when the activity is both dangerous and required by the instructor for a grade or graduation. In such cases, the instructor should use extraordinary efforts to prevent injuries from occurring.

One further item is worthy of mention. There has been a recent shift in the attitude of courts toward violence in sport and physical activity. Now courts are holding that a participant assumes the risk of injury during activity only for those actions that are an inherent part of the activity. For example, in Bourque v. Duplechin, the court found that a player did not assume the risk of intentional misconduct during sport. In this situation, Duplechin, who was a victim of a double play, ran out of the base path and into Bourque delivering a blow with his arm which caused serious injury. Bourque was entitled to recover from Duplechin for the injuries caused by his blow. A similar result occurred in Nabozny v. Barnhill, when a soccer goalie was injured by intentional contact in the "penalty area" of the field. The court held that he did not assume the risk of a kick in the head under such circumstances. In these cases, the participant causing the injury was liable for his intentional misconduct. However, if it could be shown that the coach encouraged or condoned such conduct by his players and did adequately supervise them to prevent such intentional misconduct, he might well be found negligent in his supervision of the team. These cases will be discussed further in the section dealing with assumption of the risk in sports.

STUDENT CHARACTERISTICS

A number of guidelines exist regarding the characteristics of students and how the coach or teacher must consider them during the instruction or coaching period. The activity, level of supervision, equipment, and instruction must all be considered when developing instructional materials. Advanced performers may require differing techniques and instructions than beginners. Beginners may be unaware of dangers and hazards that are known to the more advanced performer. Advanced performers may attempt more dangerous activities than beginners. These are all considerations that should be reflected in the instruction and supervision.

The students' health status and the nature of past injuries must be considered when asking them to perform physical activity. The instructor or coach is responsible to consider all of the (physical or mental) health factors that he or she either knew about, or reasonably should have known about. For example, if a student reports for balance beam instruction with a runny nose and cough, the instructor should be aware of the potential involvement of the inner ear and its subsequent influence on balancing ability. Likewise, if the student has been absent for an extended period of time with an illness or injury, the instructor reasonably should suspect that it was serious and investigate further before requiring the student to participate in class. If physicians request more information about the physical activities which are required of their patient, such information should be provided.

It is important to consider the mental attitude of participants before requiring participation in an activity. If they are fearful or apprehensive, some extra assistance should be given before they are required to participate in the activity. This consideration and the health status mentioned above are becoming more important with the inclusion of handicapped students in the physical education and athletic programs. In contrast, the coach must also weigh the desire of the athlete to return to competition as soon as possible against the seriousness of the injury or illness that caused the athlete to miss participation, and the amount of rehabilitation that may have occurred. Often highly motivated athletes desire to return to competition and practice before they are ready.

Finally, when having group activities and combatives, the teacher or coach must consider the comparable size, weight, strength, motor ability, and skill of the participants. The instructor or coach must make sure that the competitors are approximately equal in the factors above to prevent undue risk of injuries from occurring. Such equalization of competitors should occur also in athletic contests. It would be foolish to have two teams with greatly unequal size, maturity and skill competing as the risk of injury would increase greatly. The cases which provide the basis for these guidelines are summarized in Drowatzky (1977).

EQUIPMENT

A more detailed discussion of the duties associated with equipment is presented in the Products Liability chapter, but a brief mention of instructional considerations is appropriate here. The institution has the duty to provide the equipment, but the instructor or coach has the duty to inspect the equipment before use to make sure it is in good repair and safe. The instructor must also use reasonable care in the choice of equipment to make sure it is appropriate to the activity and to the students who will use it; thus, equipment must reflect the age, size and skill level of the students.

The necessary safety equipment should be present for the activity, such as face masks for softball and eye guards for racquetball. Instructions relative to safety and safety equipment should be given. The instructor must reasonably foresee dangers and take adequate precautions or provide reasonable protection from the dangers associated with equipment. Finally, the equipment must be stored in such a manner as to render the equipment harmless. If students placed the equipment in storage, the instructor has a duty to check its condition to make sure it is stored in a harmless fashion. Many of these points are mentioned above and elsewhere in this monograph, so this summary is meant to emphasize their importance.

ASSUMPTION OF THE RISK

One of the legal defenses used when injuries to sports participants have led to court action is that the participant assumed the risks associated with participation in the activity. To invoke this defence, the defendant must show that the plaintiff knew the risks involved and voluntarily assumed the risks. For many years, the doctrine of assumption of risk was broadly applied to participation in sport and recreation activities with the result that few, if any, courts imposed liability on a participant for injuries inflicted upon another. Courts did not want to "chill the vigor of athletic competition" and found it difficult to determine whether injuries were the result of intentional misconduct. However, recent trends showing increased skill and strength of participants and increased violence in sports participation have resulted in the courts extending "some of the restraints of civilization" to athletic and recreational participation. Today the majority view is that participants in an athletic event owe a duty to other participants to refrain from reckless misconduct. Today, liability may result from injuries caused a player by reason of the breach of that duty. Now courts are holding that a participant assumes the risk of injury during activity only for those actions that are an inherent part of the activity and play that is outside the rules is not an inherent part of the sport. Perhaps the following cases best illustrate the present legal view toward conduct by athletes that is outside the rules.

Bourque v. Duplechin, Nabozny v. Barnhill, and Hackbart v. Clark represent cases in which the behavior of other participants resulted in injury and liability caused by play outside the rules of the game. In Bourque v. Duplechin, the plaintiff, a second baseman, was injured when the defendant, a member of an opposing softball team, ran out of the base path when running from first to second base, to run into the plaintiff, who was standing five feet away from second base. The injury was caused by a blow delivered under the chin, and the sides were retired as a result because the collision was a flagrant violation of the rules of the game. According to testimony, Duplechin turned and ran directly at Bourque, going full speed, and did not attempt to reduce his speed or slide. The court held that Duplechin was under a duty to play softball in the ordinary fashion without unsportsmanlike conduct or causing wanton injury to his fellow players. Bourque assumed the risk of being hit by a bat or a ball and of injury resulting from standing in the base path and being spiked by someone sliding into second base, but not the risk of Duplechin going out of his way to run into him at full speed when he was five feet away from the base and standing out of the base path. In summary, the court held that ". . . a participant in a game or sport assumes all of the risks incidental to that particular activity which are obvious and foreseeable. A participant does not assume the risk from fellow players acting in an unexpected or unsportsmanlike way with a reckless lack of concern for others participating."

A similar result occurred in Nabozny v. Barnhill where the plaintiff was a goal keeper. While he was crouched on one knee controlling the ball in the penalty area, the defendant kicked him in the head and he suffered permanent damage to his skull and brain. This court stated

> . . . when athletes are engaged in athletic competition; all teams involved are trained and coached by knowledgeable personnel; a recognized set of rules governs conduct of the competition; and a safety rule is contained therein which is primarily designed to protect players from serious injury, a player is then charged with a legal duty to every other player on the field to refrain from conduct proscribed by a safety rule. A reckless disregard for the safety of other players cannot be excused.

To engage in such conduct is to create an intolerable and unreasonable risk of serious injury to other participants. . . . [A] player is liable for injury in a tort action if his conduct is such that it is either deliberate, willful or with a reckless disregard for the safety of the other player so as to cause an injury to that player.

Until recently, the courts were reluctant to impose that standard of care upon professional athletes. Hackbart v. Cincinnati Bengals, Inc., and Charles "Booby" Clark reversed this policy. Summarizing the facts involved in this case, Hackbart was playing a free safety position on the Denver Broncos' defensive team, and Charles Clark was playing fullback on the Cincinnati Bengals' offensive team. During the play when the injury occurred, Clark was in an area that was the defensive responsibility of Hackbart. A pass was intercepted by a Denver linebacker and Hackbart fell to the ground during an attempt to block Clark in the end zone. He turned and while on one knee watched the play continue up field. Clark, acting out of anger and frustration, but without specific intent to injure, struck a blow with his right forearm to the back of Hackbart's head with sufficient force to cause both players to fall forward to the ground. Following the game, Hackbart experienced pain and soreness. Later he was released on waivers and after losing his employment he sought medical assistance, at which time it was discovered he had suffered a neck injury. The trial court refused to consider the issue of negligence in professional football games.

The 10th Circuit Appellate Court reversed the trial court decision. It ruled that the appropriate standard to judge the conduct was that of recklessness and ". . . that the injuries were the result of acts of Clark which were in reckless disregard to Hackbart's safety." Recklessness was defined as existing when a person intends the act and knows that the act is harmful but fails to realize that it will produce the extreme harm which it did produce. According to this court, there are no principles of law which allow a court to rule out certain tortious conduct by reason of the general roughness of professional sports like football, or of the difficulty in administering it. The court concluded . . . "that the trial court did not limit the case to a trial of the evidence bearing on defendant's liability but rather determined that as a matter of social policy the game was so violent and unlawful that valid lines could not be drawn, we take the view that this was not a proper issue for determination and that plaintiff was entitled to have the case tried on an assessment of his rights and whether they had been violated."

If assumption of inherent risks is a viable defense, the problem for sports professionals is to show that the participants had knowledge of the risks involved in participation and voluntarily assumed the risks. Without some kind of proof, the issue becomes one person's word against another person's word. Consequently, more and more frequently, participants are asked to sign informed consent statements before they participate. These statements are often combined with release and waiver language.

WAIVERS AND INFORMED CONSENT

With increased opportunity for injury as more people participate in more physical activities more frequently, administrators have searched for methods to restrict their liability. A second factor contributing for this search to restrict liability is the increased tendency of our population to use the courts to resolve problems and to receive compensation for their troubles. Consequently, people are faced with a request to sign a release and waiver form before either they or their children can participate in sports activities. An example of the typical waiver used follows.

Some release and waiver forms also include a statement that the parents or participants will indemnify the school or association for any and all expenses occurred by an injury to the participant or spectator.

If this release were taken at face value, the Association, school, club or institution requiring the waiver would be relieved of all cost for injuries occurring during the operation of their programs. However, courts have gone to great length to void releases and waivers. In theory, for a release and waiver to be valid, the participant must have the opportunity to refuse to sign or to modify the form to be signed and still participate. Typically, such is not the case; the participant or participant's parents must sign or participation will not be permitted. Coercion such as this is taken into account by the courts when they look for ways to void the waiver or release. The typical result is shown in Doyle v. Bowdoin College v. Cooper International where the court held that agreements signed by parents were not releases of liability, and the document as executed was not an agreement of indemnity. Other courts have used differing approaches to get the same result. For example, courts held that the parents released their right to sue, but the parents could not release the rights of their child to sue. In such circumstances the parents can then bring a cause of action on behalf of the child.

If the courts do not recognize releases and waivers as removing liability, why use such devices? There are two reasons for this practice. First, informed consent is an important concept in liability determinations. If one knowingly consents to participation, or if the parents knowingly and voluntarily consent to their child's participation, the school remains responsible for its negligence. However, its liability for negligence committed by the participant is greatly reduced. Knowingly means that the person must be informed of the risks involved in participation and how the activity is conducted. The release and waiver form shown above provides all information required except what type of risks the participants face during the activity. By having a signed statement, called a release or informed consent, the institution, teacher, or coach can show exactly what the parties were told about the activity. Thus, it is important to give some descriptions of the risks involved through participation within the form. As mentioned in the product liability chapter, a duty is imposed on coaches and teachers to warn and instruct for safe use of the equipment. As described by Sales (1982), careful records will show that this duty was met.

The second reason reflects the nature of our legal system; namely, that legal requirements change with time. The courts in several cases involving adult plaintiffs who signed releases and/or waiver have held the use of such devices in the settings described was not against public policy and upheld the defendants' reliance upon them. Examples of these decisions include Banfield v. Louis (1991) and Buchan v. U.S. Cycling Federation (1991) upholding the use of a waiver/release in a bicycle race, and Williams v. Cox Enterprises (1981) involving a release signed by a runner in the Peachtree Road Race. However, generic releases that do not specify the potential injuries may not be enforceable (Macek v. Schooner's, 1991) so the consent must describe the risks likely to be present in the activity.

Two other items are worthy of mention with regard to releases and waivers. If a release is granted for one form of transportation or activity, do not change the approved activity without securing permission from the granting parties. If the parents give permission for the members of a school's basketball team to travel to the game by bus and the star player is late, do not let the assistant coach stay behind to bring the player in his car. If an auto accident should occur in which the player is killed or injured on the way to the game, and the parents have not given consent for automobile transport, the school and its employees will be liable. It would have been better to leave the star behind and give a lesson in punctuality than to have the result described above.

If medical information is going to be provided to college, university or professional athletic teams, the player should sign a release that gives permission to do so. When people serve as photographic models, they should also sign a release giving permission for use of the photo. The latter release is easy to get and can be included as a part of the release or consent form that all players sign when the season begins. However, the medical release should be signed only in those cases where it is *appropriate* rather than by all players on the team.

SUMMARY

Legal responsibilities are based on the relationship or relative status existing between parties. The person in the more powerful position has legal duties with respect to the party in the weaker position. This is particularly true with teacher-pupil, coach-athlete or doctor-patient relationships. This legal duty requires the person in the more responsible position to use due care to avoid injury to an interest of the other. Failure to use due care is called negligence when four conditions are met. These four conditions are: (1) the presence of a duty; (2) a breach of the duty; (3) an injury; and (4) the injury was caused by the breach of duty.

The standard used to determine if due care was exercised is called the reasonable person standard. The defendant's acts are compared with the mythical typical person having similar training and experience in the activity. Of course, the reasonable person used for the standard has no lapse of memory or other faults.

This chapter described standards used to judge the performance of professionals in the performance duties such as teaching or coaching or supervising activities. Inasmuch as every situation is different, every case considered will be judged individually. The professional is not required to guarantee that no injuries will occur, only that due care and reasonable actions will be used.

CHAPTER 3

FACILITIES

One characteristic of physical education and sports activities is the highly visible and attractive group of facilities associated with sport and physical activity. Not only are the facilities highly visible, they are expensive, in great demand and potentially dangerous. Thus, the supervision and maintenance of facilities are important functions of the sport and physical education professional. The increased leisure time and high interest in both participation and spectator sports create special problems in the administration of sports facilities. Larger numbers of people use, either with or without permission, playing fields, running tracks, tennis courts and other facilities. Likewise, the management and safety of large crowds attending sporting events requires extensive planning before the events occur.

OWNERSHIP OF FACILITIES

The legal system has created the concept of duty to determine and limit the extent of liability placed upon the owners and occupiers of land or facilities such as schools, sport facilities and recreational areas. Persons on the premises who are working for or acting on behalf of the owner or possessor are subject to the same liabilities and entitled to the same immunity as the owner or possessor. In general, the person in control of such property has the privilege to make use of the land for his or her own benefit and according to his or her own desires while preventing an unreasonable risk of harm to others in the area (Prosser, 1971). There are several ways that one can breach the duty to prevent unreasonable risk of harm to others. For example, the property owner may perform acts which damage adjoining land; the owner may be negligent in the care of the property; the owner may allow unusually dangerous activities to be performed on the property; or the owner may conduct activities which disturb the peace and are viewed as a nuisance.

ENTRY ONTO PROPERTY OR FACILITIES

People may enter land or property either with or without the permission of the owner or possessor. The law recognizes several classes of persons who enter land or facilities that determine the duties involved if an injury occurs on the premises of a defendant. These categories of persons are trespassing adults, trespassing children, licensees, and invitees. The act of trespass occurs when someone enters the land or facility without the permission of the owner or occupier or any of the owner's employees or agents. Those persons having permission to enter the property are classed as either licensees or invitees, depending upon the type of permission received.

CLASSES OF PEOPLE ENTERING
LAND OR PROPERTY

Without Permission
  Adult Trespass
  Child Trespass
  Foreseeable Trespass

With Permission
  Licensee
  Invitee

Adult Trespasser. According to law, the lowest duty owed by the property owner is to the adult trespasser. This person is defined as "a person who enters or remains upon land in the possession of another without a privilege to do so, created by the possessor's consent or otherwise" (Torts 2nd). Such trespassers have no right to demand a safe place and, consequently, when they enter the property the responsibility for safety is theirs and they assume the risk of whatever they encounter; they are expected to look out for themselves. However, a number of qualifications to this general rule exist.

The first important qualification relates to the situation where the property owner, or the agent, has knowledge that a substantial number of trespassers frequently enter the land at a particular point or are in the habit of traversing a small part of the land, such as is the case in the use of a path across the land. This situation imposes a burden of reasonable care to prevent injuries to such trespassers. Further, the failure to object to such trespass is considered by many courts to amount to tacit permission by the property owner and trespass no longer occurs.

The second exception occurs if the activity conducted on the premises manifests a high degree of danger to the trespassers. Under such circumstances the owner must use due care for the safety of others. Courts have usually restricted such cases to railroads and construction or blasting areas, but facility managers should recognize that the possibility for such exceptions exist.

The third and most important exception relates to discovered trespassers. It is now generally accepted that the possessor must exercise reasonable care for such a person's safety once his or her presence is known. It is not necessary that the trespasser is actually perceived, rather it is enough that the possessor is notified by information that would lead a reasonable person to conclude that a trespasser is or was there, or to proceed on that assumption. Consequently, the facility manager has the duty of reasonable care imposed regarding trespassers who sneak in to watch sports activities or to participate in activities using the facilities when it can be shown that a reasonable person should have known such trespass would occur. A warning may be sufficient unless it becomes apparent that the trespasser is insensible (Bragg v. Central New England R. Co.; Tyson v. Eastern Carolina R. R. Co.), helpless (Chicago Terminal v. Kotoski), or the warning has not been noticed or heard (Yazoo & M.V.R. Co. v. Lee; Russo v. Texas & Pac. R. Co.). Under such conditions some other action must be taken by the possessor.

Child Trespassers. The child trespasser is considered in a different category because of important developmental differences existing between children and adults. Children are immature and lack the experience and judgment of adults; they may be incapable of understanding and appreciating the possible dangers that might occur during their trespass. Society also has an interest in making land safe, within reasonable limits, to children. As a consequence the landowner has a greater burden of care toward a child trespasser than toward an adult trespasser. The landholder must therefore consider that children will trespass and evaluate how the property might be of harm to a child. In other words, the foreseeability of harm to a child is a part of the duty of the property owner or possessor that is not present for adults who trespass on the property.

> Child and foreseeable trespassers increase the duty of care required of the owner

Foreseeable Trespass. As mentioned above, in situations where the property owner can foresee that trespass will occur or when the owner has actual knowledge of trespass, the duty of care to the trespasser changes. Failure to take adequate precautions to prevent injury to trespassers in such situations will be treated as negligence and impose liability on the owner or possessor and/or agent. Once the owner either knows or should have known that trespass occurs, the owner must consider the tendency children have to meddle with interesting objects and their potential inability to understand and appreciate any danger that might exist for them. The legal system formed four conditions for liability to be imposed upon the possessor. According to the Restatement of Torts 2nd, they are:

1. The occupier of the property must have reason to anticipate the presence of the children at the place of danger. The circumstances which make the trespass foreseeable must be known to the possessor; the owner is not required to investigate or make inquiry or police the facilities unless the owner has a reasonable anticipation that trespass will occur.

2. The condition on the property must be one which the occupier should recognize as involving an unreasonable risk of harm to the children. To emphasize again, the condition must be one that the occupier either knows or should know exists; the owner is not required to inspect the land for dangers in the absence of any reasonable anticipation of trespass. In other words, the occupier is not required to insure that no danger exists on the property.

3. Liability is imposed if the child, because of immaturity, either does not discover the danger or fails to anticipate the danger involved. If the child is fully aware of the condition, understands and appreciates the risk which is present and is able to avoid the danger, then the trespassing child is treated as a trespassing adult.

4. The utility to the occupier of maintaining the present condition of the property is weighed with the risk to the children involved. Public policy with regard to property is encouraging the free use of land and avoiding the imposition of precautions that are so burdensome and unreasonable as to greatly restrict the use of the property. Thus, the owner is not required to completely "childproof" the property. The owner and agents are held to be liable for negligence only if they fail to use reasonable care and fail to take those precautions which would be taken by a reasonable person under the circumstances.

ENTRY WITH PERMISSION

As mentioned above, persons who have permission to enter the premises, either inferred or expressed, are treated differently by the law if they should suffer injury while on the property. The two most common classifications of those persons having permission to enter the premises are licensees and invitees. The following paragraphs describe the differences between the two types of persons and the difference in the legal duties owed them.

Licensees. Any person who has a privilege or "license" to enter the property is classified as a licensee. It is usually limited to those who enter the premises with the consent of the possessor. This person is not a trespasser as the individual has permission to enter the property; however, this person comes for his or her own purpose rather than for any purpose or interest of the possessor. The most common types of people classified as licensees would include persons who are taking a shortcut across the

> Licensees must be warned of known risks by the owner

property; loafers; those seeking shelter from the weather; spectators and sightseers who were not in any way invited to come; those who enter for social visits or personal visits with employees; and those soliciting money for charity. Such permission may be tacit and manifested by the defendant's conduct (i.e., they are not requested to leave when their presence is known), or by the condition of the land. Persons who use tennis courts and other facilities, but are in no way associated with the institution would also fall into this classification.

The question remains, what type of duty is owed to the licensee? Today most courts are in agreement that the possessor or operator of a facility must exercise reasonable care for the protection of the licensee. The obligation is higher than that owed to the trespasser (with the exception of the child trespasser under certain conditions listed above), because the possessor may be required to look out for the licensee before his or her presence has been discovered. Here, for example, a warning should be given as opposed to no duty to warn the trespasser. In other words, the licensee is required to accept the premises in the condition that the occupier uses them, but he is entitled to have knowledge of the risk. The licensee is not expected to assume the risk of defective stairs, slippery floors or defective electrical wiring without warning. The occupier is not required in inspect the premises for defects; the duty only arises when the occupier has actual or circumstantial knowledge of the risk. There is no duty to the licensee to maintain the premises in a safe condition, only to provide warning of known dangers.

Invitees. For those persons who enter the property upon the occupier's invitation, either express or implied, the occupier is under a duty to protect them. This affirmative duty extends not only to those dangers of which the owner knows, but also against those dangers which with reasonable care the owner might discover. Among those persons classified as invitees would be spectators, athletes, performers and officials. In most cases, the duty would also extend to independent contractors such as those providing refreshment or souvenirs. The basis for this

> Invitees must be protected from known risks and risks that would be discovered with reasonable care

liability has been stated as either the potential economic gain of the possessor or, in the alternative, a representation implied by the occupier when others are encouraged to enter to further a purpose of the owner that the facilities are safe. In both theories, the expectation is that reasonable care will be exercised to make the place safe for those who come in response. It is possible that some persons not in any way affiliated with the institution who enter the premises to use the tennis or other facilities will be viewed by some courts as invitees. It has been held that, if a city installs playground equipment and then opens it for general use, the users are invitees as the situation provides public invitation (Monfils v. City of Sterling Heights; Kelly v. Board of Education). A court may view the situation in which schools or universities open their facilities for the use by the general public in a like manner.

Participants and Officials. It is important to note that spectators, athletes and officials may be all viewed in a like manner with respect to the duty owed them by the institution. Thus, when participants, officials, and others bring legal action against the operator of facilities, the legal issue will generally be whether the operators have fulfilled their duty with regard to those using the facility. The operator will be held liable for all conditions on the premises which cause physical harm to the invitees, the participants, and officials, if the operator either knew or should have known through reasonable inspection that the condition exists and that it poses an unreasonable risk of harm which the participants, officials and others will not discover or protect themselves against. The operator must use reasonable care to protect such persons from injury caused either by the condition of the facilities, the equipment located on the premises or by the conduct of other invitee-participants, spectators, and third parties. This is not to say that the operator must insure that no harm will occur; the operator may assume, for example, that all participants will obey the rules and customs of the game. Recovery for injuries suffered at the facility will be allowed only if it can be shown that the operator breached his duty of reasonable care, and that this breach was the proximate cause of the injury.

Spectators. The presence of adequate crowd control is one aspect of safety that must be provided for participants, officials and other spectators. Indeed, most courts have held that the operator is responsible to provide for adequate crowd control and supervision. Awards to persons suffering injury or death due to mob conditions at rock concerts emphasize the principle that the operator must provide for reasonable control of crowds at the facility. Further, many athletic associations have rules which provide that a school or team will be held responsible for the conduct of its own supporters regardless of the location of the athletic event. Such rules, if they meet the requirements of reasonableness and constitutionality (see the material on rule-making in this monograph), will be supported by the courts. The primary issue here is that appropriate standards of the required conduct are present to meet the requirements of due process. If appropriate standards are provided by the association, then the school or institution will be advised of the conduct that is required by its supporters, and the punishment that will result from a failure of its fans to meet the conduct standards. See Kelly v. Metropolitan County School Board for an example of the court's requirement for pre-existing standards of conduct in such rules.

EXAMPLES OF COURT DECISIONS

The plaintiff brought this action against the University after she suffered a broken leg when she was knocked down by a drunk as she was returning to her car, parked in the University parking lot, after a watching a football game. The man who fell into her had been drinking while attending a tailgate party instead of watching the game from the stands. Finding that the University was aware of the consumption of alcoholic beverages and that tailgate parties are held in the parking lots, it is foreseeable that some people will become intoxicated and pose a general danger to other patrons. Therefore, the University was under a duty to take reasonable precautions to protect those who attend its football games from injury caused by the acts of others (Bearman v. University of Notre Dame).

Although the courts did not specifically mention the difference with which it views licensees and invitees, the following two cases from New York seem to use this approach. In the first case, a student at one of the schools in the state university system was participating in an intramural softball game on a field ordinarily used for soccer. During play, he attempted to catch a foul ball approximately 15 feet away from the third base line, stepped into a drainage ditch and injured his foot. The Appellate Division of the Supreme Court overturned a decision by the Court of Claims for the injured party and found the college was not liable. According to the court, the state was required to act reasonably in providing a field of play, and this field was adequate for its intended purpose (Scaduto v. State).

In contrast to this finding, the court in Lamphear v. State awarded an injured participant damages. This situation involved an intercollegiate softball player who was injured as she slid into third base during a regularly scheduled softball game on a makeshift softball field provided for the intercollegiate game. The field had received considerable rain, but was judged playable at the time the injury occurred. The plaintiff caught her foot in a depression near third base that was a foot wide, three inches deep, and hidden from view by grass. She was awarded $18,000 for her injury since she was participating in a normal activity for softball and had no previous knowledge of the depression.

The reason for the disparity in the courts' decisions is not readily apparent as several possibilities exist. For example, the difference may be in the classification of the plaintiffs as indicated above. The varsity athlete could have been viewed as an invitee present for the benefit of the university. In contrast, the intramural player was there for his own benefit, not that of the university. Also, the visibility of the hazard may have been a determining factor. In the intramural situation the hazard was highly visible and a dry field was involved, while in the athletic situation the danger was hidden and the field was extremely wet. In any event, these cases point up the need for using due care when providing playing areas for sports.

Proprietors and operators of facilities should install necessary safety equipment and upgrade the safety equipment in their facility as necessary or reasonably prudent. As an example, a plaintiff went to a college hockey doubleheader at a state facility in New York. He left his seat for the concession area and while returning decided to watch the rest of the game from the area of the player's bench. No protective fencing was installed in front of the player's bench, and he was struck in the head by an errant puck. During the court hearing, testimony was provided that it was customary to provide protective fencing by the player's bench. If fencing is not provided, it creates a zone of danger, and spectators are not allowed to be in those areas. Consequently, the court found that the lack of a protective fence in the area produced a dangerous condition that presented a foreseeable risk of injury to any spectators who happened to sit in the area where the plaintiff was seated (Benjamin v. State).

The need to upgrade the safety features in the facility when reasonable is illustrated in the next two cases. In the first case, Eddy v. Syracuse University, a university student was playing a game of frisbee at the end of the gymnasium having glass doors. During the course of the game the student ran through the doors, suffering severe lacerations to his arm. The court held that the University should have foreseen that on such a gymnasium as was present, students would use the gymnasium area for impromptu, unique and novel games. The glass doors not only held a danger for such students, but also for the basketball players and other users. The University had a duty to protect the users of the gymnasium from such harm. A similar situation and finding occurred in Wilkinson v. Hartford Accident and Indemnity Company. Here the plaintiff and several classmates went to the lobby for a drink during a physical education class in which they were running relay races. While in the lobby they decided to race for positions on the next relay, and the plaintiff pushed on a glass pane while running at full speed; he fell through the glass and suffered severe cuts and loss of blood. After the accident the school board installed safety glass in the panel. The Supreme Court of Louisiana found the school board guilty of negligence for failing to install or replace the non-safety glass in the lobby area. Most courts view the replacement of non-safety glass with safety glass as a reasonable expectation.

Railings and similar safety equipment are viewed in a similar manner. In Woodring v. Board of Education a workman in a gymnasium was attempting to get onto a platform from a step ladder. During his movement he grabbed the railing around the platform, which gave way causing him to fall to his death. The cause of failure was due to the fact that a required nut and bolt were not in place to secure the railing. The school was held liable as it had no program of preventative maintenance or inspection, and the installation of the railing was not in accordance with proper construction practice. The court added that, since the platform was used extensively in school functions and that students were known to hang from the railing and do somersaults, it was foreseeable that injury would occur if it was not properly installed and maintained.

Outdoor facilities, in addition to playing fields described above, must be inspected for safety. A high school student was cut when he fell while jogging on an outdoor track. Broken glass was present on the track and had not been noticed or cleared. The plaintiff argued that the school staff had a duty to inspect the track and supervise the custodial staff to make sure the premises were maintained in a safe condition; their failure to do so produced his injury. The court agreed with his argument and held the coach, athletic director, or supervisor of grounds were liable (Short v. Griffitts).

SUMMARY

This chapter summarized the legal duties and obligations of owners, operators and proprietors of sport and physical education facilities. Such persons are held accountable the same as is any property owner. In some few situations the state or school board may not be liable for injuries because of the concept of governmental immunity, but the person responsible for the supervision and operation of facilities does not have such immunity. Also, most states have eliminated the concept of governmental immunity; thus, one should not count on the presence of this doctrine for protection. As is the case in all legal situations, the extent of one's duty depends upon all the facts and circumstances.

Among the factors determining the duty is the status of the person entering the property. Unless there is an unusually dangerous activity being conducted on the property, or the property owner has knowledge of someone entering the property, he has no obligation to provide for the safety of those persons entering the property without permission. There is some modification to this general rule for the child trespasser, however. Two classes of persons having permission to enter the property were described, the licensee and the invitee. The highest duty of care is owed to the invitee.

Finally, the duty of reasonable care involves the facilities, the equipment located on the premises, and third parties. The operator must exercise adequate control of spectators and others who are present at the event. When new safety features become available at a reasonable price and become the new standard, the facility operator should upgrade the present facilities; the best example of this situation is the replacement of non-safety glass with safety glass in areas where it is reasonable to expect injury from glass. The operator, or agents, should also inspect the premises for dangerous conditions such as the absence of adequate safety railings and the presence of broken glass. If such conditions exist, they must be quickly corrected. It is important to remember that the responsibility of the operator for safety in construction does not end when the facility is completed. Preventive maintenance and other similar operations are also required. The use of inspection and other check sheets are helpful in meeting these duties.

CHAPTER 4

PERSONNEL MANAGEMENT

It may be that most of the time spent by administrators of sport and physical education programs relates to dealings with personnel. While the administrator may have the overall responsibility for facilities and the other aspects of the program, it is the personnel under the administrator to whom these tasks are delegated. This administrative responsibility is not limited to those persons who are employed by the school or institution, but also extends to others who come in contact with the athletic or physical activity programs: students, spectators, officials, medical personnel, trespassers, athletes and visitors to the facilities. Many of the legal duties relating to these classes of people are discussed in other chapters describing negligence, facilities, sport medicine and product liability. This chapter, consequently, will focus on employer-employee relationships, rule-making and control of athletes or others, and the relationships of school or institution to conference or association.

EMPLOYER-EMPLOYEE RELATIONSHIPS

A task common to most administrators is the hiring and supervision of those persons who report to them according to the administrative structure. Therefore, the courts universally hold that administrators must use due care in the selection and supervision of persons who work under their direction. The administrator must make sure the employees are qualified by education and experience, and then make periodic evaluations to make sure that they are performing as required. If any employees are deficient in their performance, the administrator must take reasonable corrective action to have them perform as required. Failure on the part of the administrator to exercise due care in the selection and supervision of personnel will result in negligence. The administrator is responsible for following the institutional guidelines that pertain to the job and also for all the state and federal legislation that has been enacted with respect to hiring and retention of employees and availability of the programs to others. Today all public institutions and many private institutions receiving public funds must affirm a policy of equal opportunity and have an affirmative action policy that they follow. This policy must reflect the following legislative actions and executive orders.

- Executive Order 11246/Revised Order #4 (as amended by 11375 and 11141) as amended
- The Equal Pay Act of 1963
- The Equal Employment Act of 1972
- Titles VI and VII of the Civil Rights Act of 1964, as amended by the Equal Employment Act of 1972, the Pregnancy Discrimination Act of 1976, as amended in 1979, and Guidelines for Sexual Harassment established in 1980
- The Family Education Rights and Privacy Act of 1974 and Freedom of Information Act of 1964
- Sections 503 and 504 of the Rehabilitation Act of 1973
- Public Law 94-142, Education for All Handicapped Children of 1975
- Title IX of the 1972 Education Amendment of the Higher Education Act
- Section 402 of the Vietnam Era Veterans Readjustment Assistance Act of 1974
- The Age Discrimination in Employment Act of 1967
- Americans with Disabilities Act of 1991
- Sections in the appropriate State Revised Code

This monograph is too limited in space to describe all the requirements contained in these orders and acts, so you should check with your institution and get a copy of the pertinent materials. Also, the rules and regulations issued to accompany these orders or acts are periodically reviewed and modified. In most cases the *Congressional Record* has printed them, and you can get a copy of that document by writing to the appropriate governmental office and requesting the rules and regulations. The point is that the administrator has a large task keeping current with such requirements, completing the necessary reports, and performing certain other tasks required in these acts and orders.

No entirely satisfactory legal definition of the term "contract" exists. However, every contract involves at least one promise that has legal consequences. The most widely quoted definition is that "A contract is a promise, or a set of promises, for breach of which the law gives a remedy, or the performance of which the law in some way recognizes as a duty" (Wiliston, 1907). Perhaps a better approach is to regard a contract as a legally enforceable agreement, although some things may be enforceable without agreement. In most school or institutional settings, employment is based on a written contract or certificate of appointment that must be signed by the employee and the person who has the legal power to complete such agreements for the institution. This person is usually the President acting after the Board of Trustees, Board of Education, or a similar body has given official approval. Such written contracts and agreements may specify the duties and responsibilities of the parties, or they may be incorporated into agreement by such language as . . . "Services shall be rendered in accordance with pertinent provisions of the Revised Code of Ohio, the Bylaws and established policies of the Board of Trustees, the rules of the University, and such other special conditions, if any, specifically set forth below" (Certificate of Appointment, The University of Toledo, Ohio). In this situation all of the documents mentioned become a part of the agreement regardless of whether the employee has taken the time to read them. In addition to the written form, contracts may be verbal, or in some cases the courts will imply that a contract exists (Calmari & Perillo, 1970). The contract is a form used to establish legal duties between the employer and employee. These duties may be modified by subsequent agreements that amend the original contract. A large body of law relating to contracts has been developed, and administrators should consult the attorney representing their institution if questions arise about such matters.

Athletic regulation in private schools is usually approached using private law principles contained in contract law. This is true for relationships between the athlete and school, as well as that between the school and association or conference. When such private relationships are formed, the rules and regulations specified by or incorporated into the agreement are binding, and disputes must be resolved following those procedures courts will intervene only in exceptional cases.

In the case of the public schools, public law principles will be applied by the courts, and there is less judicial reluctance to intervene in such situations. In these situations appropriate private law principles may be applied, but first the court will see if all constitutional provisions that apply are met and will investigate such delegated authority from the legislature to the schools to make sure that the schools did not exceed it. After these steps are completed, then private law will be applied if it is applicable. In a landmark decision (Goss v. Lopez), the U.S. Supreme Court held that public education was a property right, and students cannot be permanently expelled from school. However, participation in extracurricular activities remains a privilege rather than a right, and students may be denied participation for appropriate reasons. It is important to note that recently the judicial attitude has been one of increasingly moving toward intervention, so the administrator must make sure all actions are done as should be done.

Agency Law. Agency law has evolved over the past several years until today it recognizes that employees are agents having the function of doing business for their employer or principal. The recognition of this legal relationship has effected the tort doctrine as expressed in the chapter discussing negligence. Agency law recognizes that the agent may represent the principal and affect the principal's legal relations, making the principal liable and creating rights in the principal, within the limits of, but not beyond, the agent's "authority" (Latty & Frampton, 1977). In other words, the principal may become liable for the negligent acts of the agent that occur within the scope of the agent's employment, and the agent owes the principal a fiduciary duty to act in the principal's best interest all the while functioning within the scope of employment.

Furthermore, the principal is not liable for every tort which the agent commits, but only those which are closely enough related to the risks which the principal assumed to make it fair to impose liability on the principal. In other words, the action in question must be deemed to be within the scope of employment. In other words, the scope of employment is related to reasonable expectations of the employer and is defined in the Restatement of Agency, Second.

Section 228:
1. Conduct of a servant is within the scope of employment if, but only if:

    (a) it is of the kind he is employed to perform;
    (b) it occurs substantially within the authorized time and space limits;
    (c) it is actuated, at least in part, by a purpose to serve the master; and
    (d) if force is intentionally used by the servant against another, the use of force is not unexpected by the master.

2. Conduct of a servant is not within the scope of employment if it is different in kind from that authorized, far beyond the authorized time or space limits, or too little actuated by a purpose to serve the master.

Agency law looks at the employer-employee relationship as being composed of reciprocal duties. The employer is expected to provide a safe working place, and also to use due care to inform the agent of risks of physical harm or pecuniary loss which the principal has reason to know exist in performance of authorized acts and which the principal has reason to know are unknown to the agent. The employer's duty to give other information depends upon the agreement between the two. In the case of loss during employment, the agent is entitled to indemnity from the employer, or if the agent suffers harm because of the employer's breach of his duties.

The agent or employee has a fiduciary duty with regard to the employer. According to this standard, the employee must act in the best interest of the employer. The employee has a duty to use reasonable efforts to give the employer information which is relevant to the affairs entrusted to the agent. Likewise, the agent has a duty not to disclose to others trade secrets, written lists of names or other similar confidential matters given to the agent only; to account for profits made by the sale or use of such material; and to not take advantage of a still-existing, confidential relation created during the prior agency relation. According to the Restatement of Agency, Second, an agent is subject to a duty to obey all reasonable directions and not to act in matters entrusted to him or her on account of the principal contrary to the directions of the principal, even though the terms of the employment prescribe that such directions shall not be given. Unless otherwise agreed upon, the agent has a duty to act with the standard of care and with the skill which is standard in the locality for the kind of work which the agent is employed to perform and, in addition, to exercise any special skill that he or she possess. To sum the duties of an agent or employee, Restatement of Agency, Second, Section 387 states, "Unless otherwise agreed, an agent is subject to a duty to his principal to act solely for the benefit of the principal in all matters connected with his agency."

LIABILITY FOR AGENTS' TORTS		
Conscious Assumption of Liability	**Justifiable Reliance**	**Vicarious Liability from Inherent Power**
results if an employer authorizes conduct by an employee which constitutes a tort to a third person; the employer is liable.	results through a holding out or course of prior dealing, when a third party relies on a principal's or employer's responsibility for the acts of agents which cause harm.	imposed on an employer in situations because of certain policy determinations by courts which justify its imposition without either consent or misleading actions by the principal, i.e., run-of-the-mill automobile accidents.

In summary, agency is a relationship which is variously described as being representative, fiduciary, voluntary, and consensual, and usually contractual. It is a legal relation, characterized by the power of the agent to act on behalf of the principal with third parties. The right of the principal to control the conduct of the agent with respect to matters entrusted to the agent is the test of agency and constitutes an essential element or characteristic of the agency relation.

Independent Contractor. Some administrators, upon learning that using an independent contractor does not impose the same duties and liabilities as are present with agency law, have subsequently written agreements describing many working relationships with people they hire as that existing between an independent contractor and school. However, the courts will look beyond the written agreement and see how the parties relate to each other when determining their legal relationship.

Generally the distinction between the relation of principal and agent and employer and independent contractor is based on the extent of the control exercised over the employee in the performance of the work. The worker being classified as an independent contractor if the will of the employer is represented only by the result, but an agent in situations where the employer's will is represented by control of the means as well as the result. (See Chester v. World Football League and Brown v. Wichita State University.)

AGENCY	INDEPENDENT CONTRACTOR
Employer controls means and result	Employer controls only the result
Work is part of the regular business of the principal	Work is not part of the regular business
Payment is by the time	Payment is by the job
Employer supplies the instrumentalities and tools	Employer does not supply the instrumentalities and tools

Other commonly used tests for agency include: the place of work; the time of employment; the length of time for which the services are to be performed; the skill involved; and the right to hire and discharge or otherwise terminate the relationship. After performing these tests, the courts will hold that either an agency or an independent contractor relationship exists. An employee for whose torts an employer is vicariously liable is an agent. If an employee is an agent, then the employer is a principal. If the employee is determined not to be one for whom the law will hold the employer vicariously liable, the employee is an independent contractor.

Administrative Law. Today, administrators must be involved with various governmental agencies in the performance of their duties. When this situation occurs, it is necessary to know and understand the principles of administrative law. Administrative law is concerned with the powers and procedures of administrative agencies, especially judicial review or administrative action. An administrative agency is a governmental authority, other than a court and legislative body, which affects the rights of private parties through such processes as adjudication, rule-making, investigation, prosecuting, negotiating, settling, or informal actions. These authorities are commonly called commissions, boards, authorities, agencies, bureaus, offices, officer, administrator, department, corporation, administration, or division. The complex of methods by which such agencies carry out their tasks is called the administrative process. The main point to be made is that, if you must interact with such an authority, you must become familiar with its rules, regulations and procedures. You must exhaust the administrative process before you can seek relief in the courts; the courts will require you follow all the steps specified and exhaust all the administrative options before they will accept your case. Get a copy of the appropriate legislative acts and the agency rules before you become involved in the process (Davis, 1972).

RULES AND RULE-MAKING

In the United States, the governmental rule-making procedure has been formalized and follows the democratic principle. It has been called one of the greatest inventions of modern government as it is both democratic and efficient. Schools and units comprising the schools could do well to follow the rule-making procedure used by other agencies. The pertinent procedures are as follows: 1) all persons who are or may be interested are notified; 2) tentative rules are

27

published and written comments about them received before the rules are adopted; 3) all interested parties are allowed to participate in the adoption process; 4) the administrator who is developing a set of rules is allowed to consult informally with anyone who is in a position to help; 5) retroactive rule-making can and should be avoided and 6) supervision of the rule makers is provided (Davis, 1972).

Once the rules are developed and adopted, the following principles should be followed. Notice should be given to all persons to whom the rules apply. The notice should be conspicuous, give clear standards of the conduct that is regulated, explain the requirements of the rule, and explain all penalties that will be received if the rules are broken. The rules must fall within the scope of the authority of the administrator and a reasonable relationship between the rule and its purpose must be present. The penalty contained in the rules must not be arbitrary or excessive, and there must be no constitutional impairments. The administrator should also give notice of procedural due process in which a notice of the intention to discipline is given; the person has a hearing where the charges can be rebutted; and an impartial hearing can be obtained within the school or institution. It is sound administrative policy to follow the procedures explained above whenever rule-making occurs, and whenever people are subject to discipline for a failure to conform to the rules. In the case of limited penalties, such as a letter of reprimand, the due-process procedure can be informal; if the penalty can be severe, such as expulsion or termination of employment, the due-process procedure should be formal. Coaches often establish rules for athletes to follow. They should give notice, show a reasonable relationship to the purpose, demonstrate proper exercise of authority, have penalties that are not arbitrary or excessive, and provide due process.

REGULATION OF ATHLETES

As explained earlier, private schools and public schools are often treated differently by the courts. Private schools are subjected to private law principles which look at the relationship formed and view the specified rules and procedures as binding. Public law principles, which involve looking at the constitutional provisions that apply and the delegated authority from the legislation, are applied to the public schools. Courts are less reluctant to intervene in the public schools. In all situations there has been an increase in litigation where athletes have sought to challenge the authority of schools and associations, and where schools challenge associations of which they are members. Types of rules commonly developed to regulate the conduct of athletes include: good conduct rules; amateur standing; participation in non-approved events; longevity; transfer of residence; grades; sex; marriage; race and drugs. All of these types of rules have been challenged in the courts, and the following general principles are a summary of the results of such disputes.

Athletes have a right to education, but participation in extracurricular events remains a privilege. This is not to say that athletes can be arbitrarily denied the privilege of participation, however. Organizations have substantial freedom to regulate athletic activity, but the athlete, particularly in public schools, has a "zone of interest" that may not be unreasonably impaired. Courts attempt to strike a balance between the respective interests of the athletes and the organizations which are responsible for regulating competitive activity.

Rules and regulations which are sought to be imposed on athletes will be enforced so long as they are within the authority of the adopting organization, and so long as they are adopted pursuant to a proper procedure and are proper exercises of authority. If these rules are broken, and if administrative action is taken with respect to an athlete, the action must be in accord with the requirements of procedural, due process of the law, and any determination made by an

28

administrative organization will be subjected to judicial review. At a minimum, this due process must include:

1. Notice with a statement of charges.

2. An impartial hearing with the ability to confront witnesses.

3. A written or taped transcript of the hearing.

4. Review by an impartial hearing officer.

In order for the courts to consider a rule to be an appropriate regulation of the athlete, it must meet specific standards. First, the rule-maker must be able to demonstrate that undesirable consequences of the regulated conduct are either likely to exist or have been present in the past. Next, the regulation must be shown to be a reasonable exercise of authority in the sense that it impacts only those whose conduct it is necessary to control. In other words, the regulation must be narrowly drawn, not overly broad. Finally, it must be shown that the rule is constitutional. Courts generally accept objectives of rules for athletes such as to prevent the exploitation of athletes, to promote the overall development of athletes, to equalize the competitive opportunities in athletes, and to promote the safety, health and well-being of athletes.

GOOD CONDUCT RULES

Good conduct rules relating to alcohol, participation in assaultive conduct, and lack of proper grooming have been challenged in the courts. Generally, "hair and grooming" rules and "beer" rules have been overturned because the coaches made the rules too broad. For example, an athlete in Bugger v. Iowa High School Association would lose six weeks of eligibility if he possessed, consumed or transported alcoholic beverages or dangerous drugs. The same penalty was applied if an athlete were present in a car containing any of those substances when stopped by a police officer. In the present case, an athlete was present in such a car and, although the charges against him were later dismissed, he was declared ineligible for the six-week period. He brought suit against the school requesting reinstatement on the team with no loss of eligibility. The court, using constitutional standards, found the rule to be unacceptable because the physical presence of an athlete in a car containing an alcoholic beverage, even when out of season, simply has no relation to the athletic program. Further, the rule was unreasonable because it was overly inclusive and penalized the guilty and non-guilty alike.

DRUG TESTING

The National Collegiate Athletic Association (NCAA) responded in 1986 to mounting concern about the use of drugs in college athletics by instituting a testing program for six categories of banned drugs. The purpose of this drug testing program was to provide clean, equitable competition for student athletes. Student athletes are required to sign drug testing consent forms at the beginning of each school year or they are ineligible to compete in intercollegiate games that determine eligibility for post season competition and NCAA championships. The testing protocols are modeled on those used by the United States and the International Olympic Committees. Athletes have filed complaints alleging that the drug testing program violates their right to privacy and/or constitutes an "unreasonable" search. In the California case, Hill v. NCAA, the California courts held that the drug testing program violated the student athletes' right of privacy guaranteed under the California Constitution. The California decision is a narrow decision that applies only to California because of the way its constitution is written. In contrast, the Massachusetts courts held in Bally v. Northeastern University that neither the

Massachusetts State Civil Rights Act nor the Massachusetts right of privacy statute was violated. This case is more representative of the nation as a whole as other decisions involving high school and college athletes have mirrored it.

Northeastern University's drug testing program was instituted to: (a) promote the health and physical safety of student athletes; (b) promote fair intrateam and intercollegiate competition; and (c) ensure that Northeastern student athletes, as role models to other students and as representatives to the public, are not perceived as drug users. Standardized drug collection and testing procedures were adopted to ensure the athlete submitted his or her own urine to be

> DRUG TESTING PROGRAMS
> Appropriate Purpose
> Standard Procedures
> Confidentiality
> Education Program
> Follow-up Testing
> Appeal Process

tested, confidentiality was maintained and positive tests were reevaluated. If the second test was also positive, the student athlete is notified and requested to confer with the director of the university's health center and student health services. The director decides whether to begin counseling the student. The student is given follow-up testing. If a follow-up test is negative, the individualized process ends and the student is simply once again subject to further testing like all other athletes. If a follow-up test is positive, further measures are taken, including notification of the coach, suspension from the team and attendance at a formal drug counseling program. At any point in the process, the student may appeal to the university's drug testing review and appeals committee.

One manner in which the issue of illegal search and seizure can be overcome is for the individual being tested to consent to the action. As indicated above, this approach is more commonly being used by universities when implementing a drug testing program. Courts have consistently held that in order for consent to be obtained, it must meet the criteria of being voluntary and that the individual knows the consequences of his or her actions. Whether such consent has occurred depends upon the facts and circumstances surrounding each case. Circumstances considered relevant to the question of whether consent has been obtained include age, education level, intelligence, the presence or absence of advice concerning constitutional rights and the absence of coercion forcing one to trade government benefits for constitutional rights.

While courts have consistently held that participation in athletics and other extracurricular events is a privilege rather than a right, current developments make collegiate sports participation become considerably more important to the student athletes than perhaps in times past. Consider the current salaries that are paid to athletes in professional sports such as baseball, basketball, football and hockey. Amateurs in track and field also can amass considerable income through their athletic participation. The huge amounts of money associated with athletic participation at these levels make it difficult to believe current scholar athletes accept the idea it is only a privilege to participate in sport competitions. If you are an exceptional athlete, with an excellent chance to participate at the professional level after exemplary intercollegiate participation, do you truly have the option not to sign the consent for drug testing? This question was answered in O'Halloran v. University of Washington when the court stated, "Neither does this denial of intercollegiate eligibility constitute coerced consent to the testing. There has been no showing that withholding of eligibility for intercollegiate competitions is something that a university of the NCAA may not do under any circumstances. Certainly low grades, failure to use protective athletic equipment, or medical reasons could result in the withdrawal of such eligibility." (at 1055)

Therefore, today courts view drug testing when it is a part of a drug prevention program as a satisfactory prerequisite to athletic participation. This program, summarized in the Bally decision, must include education, confidentiality and due process. Programs that include drug prevention and education as a part of their program and provide adequate safeguards will be able to implement drug testing for their athletes. The exception to this general rule is the state of California as that state constitution has been held to preclude such testing programs.

ADMINISTRATIVE DUE PROCESS

In Behagen v. Intercollegiate Conference of Faculty Representatives, a basketball player was immediately dismissed from further collegiate competition for his violence toward another opposing player during a basketball contest. He brought suit stating that he had great educational and economic interest in his continued participation and should not be prevented from

> DUE PROCESS REQUIREMENTS
> Notice
> Impartial Hearing
> Verbatim Transcript
> Impartial Review

participation that would enhance his position in the professional draft. The court reviewed the case and found that the interest of a collegiate player participating in athletics is sufficiently substantial so that it cannot be impaired without proceedings that meet the minimum requirements of procedural due process. Other courts have taken similar positions with regard to rules and disciplinary proceedings.

From this discussion it should be apparent that the athlete is subject to the supervision and direction of the coach. This authority is limited to those aspects of the athlete's life which relate directly to his or her athlete performance. The coach's authority includes the power to establish and maintain health and training rules, to direct and conduct practice sessions, and to issue reasonable instructions during competition which the athlete will accept and follow without question. This authority also encompasses the coach's ability to impose penalties for the violation of such instructions. The coach does not have the power to regulate, however, those aspects of the athlete's life that do not directly relate to athletic performance. In Dunham v. Pulsifer the court, after invalidating a hair rule, stated, "[a] coach may not demand obedience to a rule which does not in some way further other proper objectives of participation and performance." Athletic directors and coaches should evaluate the rules and regulations relating to athletes and make sure they meet the tests described above.

CONFERENCES AND ASSOCIATIONS

The general principles relating to either the school and/or athlete relative to conferences and associations have already been described above. These relationships have both constitutional and non-constitutional aspects. To pass the constitutional test, the regulation must not take away any constitutional privilege and, in the non-constitutional test, it must be shown that the activity is within the scope of the association's authority and that it is a reasonable exercise of that authority. The school or athlete must exhaust all of the administrative procedures that are contained in the agreement before the courts will accept the case for a determination. The rule-making procedures that were detailed above should be followed by associations and conferences when they establish new rules and regulations. This section is appropriate for administrators and regulators at all levels.

SUMMARY

It seems appropriate to summarize this chapter with a series of practical recommendations for administrators at all levels. These are as follows.

1. Keep your staff informed and communicate effectively. Develop manuals, have regular staff meetings, and send appropriate memos.

2. Be responsive to staff needs; you are responsible for their safety and well-being. If they inform you of problems, which is their legal duty as an agent, investigate and take appropriate action. Do not remain inactive and attempt to ignore the problems; they will not go away.

3. Commit your agreements to writing and live up to them. It is true that sometimes written agreements can be a nuisance, but they serve to protect both parties.

4. Keep good records. Send follow-up, confirming letters with dates and discussion topics to develop records of important telephone and other oral conversations.

5. Keep up to date on personal matters. Remember you are responsible for reasonable care in the selection and supervision of your personnel. Keep personnel files up to date showing commendations and disciplinary actions. Such records will help show what has transpired if you should be involved in some personnel action that is challenged.

6. Take rule-making seriously. Follow the procedures recommended in this chapter. Involve people who will be affected in the rule-making procedure. After the rules are accepted, publish them and make sure all interested parties have copies of the rules. Discard old, inappropriate rules.

7. Make sure employment contracts are written to convey all the conditions that you feel are necessary. In the high school setting, for example, some joint teaching-coaching contracts have been held to make the two positions severable while others have not. Determine how you want the position to be considered and get legal help to make sure the contract reflects that position. It is much better to plan ahead than to have to try to resolve problems that develop from inadequate documents.

8. Make sure that regulations used to control an athlete's behavior are appropriate and regulate only those aspects of the athlete's life that directly relate to his or her participation and competition. The coach's right to control athletes is narrowly drawn and should not be exceeded.

CHAPTER 5

EQUIPMENT AND SIMILAR PRODUCTS

Sport and physical education participation requires the use of equipment, sometimes extensively and sometimes minimally. In some cases the equipment is furnished by the performer, and in other cases the equipment is furnished by the school, club or some other equipment-supplier. If the performer supplies his or her own equipment, such as a varsity athlete supplying a tennis racquet, any problems resulting from the equipment are usually between the athlete and the supplier or manufacturer. The coach or teacher may have no greater role than to recommend that the athlete speak to a lawyer or the supplier. However, when sports such as football or gymnastics requiring the use of considerable equipment are involved, the school, club, or other agency usually has more extensive involvement. This occurs because typically the school, club, or other agency provides such expensive equipment to the participants.

The discussion in this chapter will be directed toward the situations in which the school either supplies sport equipment to athletes, students and other parties without charge or when a lessee-lessor arrangement is involved. The concepts of product liability and strict tort will also be discussed, and the current status of the situation surrounding the football helmet will be used as an example. Finally, legislation designed to protect consumers and users of products, the Uniform Commercial Code, will be discussed as it relates to these issues.

SCHOOLS AS SUPPLIERS

The underlying theme of this monograph has been that whenever a person, agency or institution enters into a relationship with another party, a legal obligation is present, requiring the use of due care to prevent unreasonable risk of harm. Thus, whenever the institution supplies equipment without charge to those participating in its programs, it has the duty to exercise reasonable care to supply equipment that is in a safe and suitable condition to meet the purposes for which it was intended. The equipment provided must also be appropriate to the age, maturation, and skill level of those who will use it. Therefore, the practice of handing down used high school varsity equipment for use in elementary school physical education classes in not necessarily wise. The institution is not required to insure that no harm will occur to the users; liability will attach only when a failure to perform the duty of reasonable care produces an injury.

The school has an obligation to provide appropriate and safe equipment for physical education instruction, but it is not under a legal obligation to hire individuals who will perform periodic inspections or determine the appropriateness of the equipment. That responsibility falls upon the physical education instructor or coach who, because of a contractual agreement, becomes an agent of the school board. As a consequence, when the instructor purchases equipment, the instructor must make sure that it is appropriate. When the instructors plan to use the equipment in their instruction, the instructor must inspect both the equipment and facilities for defects or breakage before use. When manufacturers provide warnings such as shown later in the chapter, instructors must teach the dangers described during use of the equipment to their students or athletes.

The principles surrounding the supply of athletic equipment to athletes are summarized by Vendrell v. School District. This case involved an injury to a high school football player who used protective equipment although he knew that "it was just a bit loose." The school in the law suit provided the football equipment without charge and gave instructions to the players regarding selection and fitting of the protective equipment. His helmet later developed a crack, and he selected a replacement from several others that were available. The court found that the school was not liable for several reasons. The coaches taught the players how to fit, inspect and use the equipment. The players were free to, at any time, return any of the equipment and select a substitute. According to the court findings, the plaintiff was intimately familiar with the suitability or unsuitability of the equipment and voluntarily decided to continue to use the equipment that he had selected.

To summarize, certain specific steps are recommended for schools who supply equipment without charge. First, make sure that the equipment selected is appropriate for the activity as well as the age, maturity, and skill of the participants. Second, inspect the equipment and facilities before use. Third, teach the participants how to fit, use and inspect the equipment. If the participants are incapable of performing these functions, then the instructors or coaches must perform these duties. Fourth, encourage the players to return any of the equipment and select a substitute at any time and to point out all breakage or defects. If the equipment receives heavy use, or is susceptible to breakage, have regularly scheduled, periodic inspections as a part of practice. At the completion of the season, the equipment should be inspected before it is returned to storage. Make all necessary repairs at this time.

Schools have also escaped liability for injuries suffered when the participants fail to wear the prescribed safety equipment (Hanna v. State), if instructions and other features mentioned above were present. Whenever participants are observed without proper equipment, the coaches and teachers should not ignore the situation. They should take corrective action. Liability is sure to result when defective equipment is provided (Rivera v. Board of Education) or when there is a lack of proper equipment for the participants (Diker v. City of St. Louis Park; Fein v. Board of Education).

Lessors of Equipment

When a lessor-lessee relationship is present, the situation is different than that described above, and the liability changes somewhat to reflect this difference. In this circumstance, the lessor will be liable for taking specific notice and account of the lease agreement. If the lessor knows, or should have known, that the equipment leased is, or is likely to be, dangerous for the purpose for which is it to be used, then liability will be imposed on the lessor if the lessor fails to use reasonable care to either make it safe for such use, or to disclose its actual condition to those who will probably use the equipment. Further, the lessor is required to inspect the equipment for defects and to properly maintain and repair the equipment leased. Once again, the lessor is not expected to insure that no injury will occur, but is liable only for those injuries caused by the lessor's negligent acts or omissions.

In view of this principle, the school, agency, or institution should provide detailed information about the actual and probable uses of equipment when it is requesting bids. Pertinent characteristics of the potential users should also be described. Actual knowledge of probable uses and users by the lessor will shift the liability for improper equipment to the lessor from the lessee, unless the lessee is told of the defects or inappropriateness and decides to use the equipment anyway. The use of a lease can also relieve the institution of some of the maintenance and inspection requirements regarding athletic equipment. This type of arrangement does not relieve coaches and teachers of their duty to provide instructions and to use good sense in the removal of equipment that breaks during use, or other acts that can be performed to remove unreasonable risk of injury.

PRODUCT LIABILITY

Product liability is the concept used to describe the case law developed in the area involving liability of sellers and producers of chattels to third persons with whom there is no privity of contract (Prosser, 1971; pp. 641–682). In earlier and simpler times, actions for product negligence was based on the requirement of privity of contract between the buyer and seller. This was based on the idea that liability for injury caused to any and all persons was too much burden to place on manufacturers and sellers of goods produced and sold. This was especially true for injuries to parties at a "distance" from retailers and with whom there was no contract. However, as goods and technology became more complex and sophisticated, social philosophy also changed, and our current ideas of responsibility for products and services produced or marketed has also changed. The state of the legal situation is as described by Noel & Phillips (1974, p. 4):

"The supplier of a product, if he fails to use due care in its manufacture or distribution, is liable to any person who is foreseeably injured by the supplier's negligent conduct. Such a person might be a purchaser, a purchaser's employee, a donee, or relative, a passerby at the time of the accident, or a bailee, licensee, or lessee of the product. No sale or rental need be involved. So when a teacher was injured because of a mislabeled free sample, the distributor was held liable. Pease v. Sinclair Ref. Co., 104 F. 2d 183 (2d Cir. 1939) (N. Y. law)."

As the above quotation indicates, once a product has been manufactured and placed into the stream of commerce, the manufacturer is responsible for any injuries caused by prior negligent conduct. This concept has been extended to others involved in the sale and distribution of goods and services also.

Nature and Extent of Duty. Consequently, today all manufacturers must use due care in the design and production of their products, comply with all governmental regulations, and employ the best of safety devices. They must also make reasonable inspections and tests of their products. Whenever dangers are unavoidable, the manufacturer has a duty to warn the inexpert user and provide proper instructions. This latter requirement is important in the present football helmet situation as evidenced by the warning shown in the following material. These duties are not removed even if a seller or some other party has either the opportunity or obligation to inspect the goods for defects.

With vendors or retailers, the general rule is that they are not liable for harm caused to third parties by a dangerous product, even though they could have discovered the condition by inspection. However, if the dealer should fail to exercise reasonable care if the dealer undertakes to make repairs on a product, the dealer will be liable for any negligence. The situation with regard to liability changes should the seller make a misrepresentation of the product. If the seller makes an erroneous statement on which the injured party justifiably relies, the seller will be held liable for negligent misrepresentation. It makes no difference whether the seller actually knew the statement was erroneous or if there was no valid reason to believe the statement was true (Restatement of Torts 2nd. Section 401). It is also immaterial as to when the statement was made, so long as the injured party can show that he or she relied on the misrepresentation. Liability for negligent misrepresentation has also been extended to certifiers of products such as independent testing agencies. Suppliers of services, although not retailers, have been held liable for negligent servicing. As this section indicates, negligence is one basis of finding liability for injuries caused from products or services placed into commerce.

Strict Liability. Strict liability, or strict tort, is a second way that liability for injuries resulting from products or services may be fixed. The major case recognizing this theory was

Greenman v. Yuba Power Products. That court imposed strict liability on the manufacturer as being in the best interests of the injured consumer. The court reasoned . . . "the purpose of such liability is to insure that the costs of injuries resulting from defective products are borne by the manufacturers that put such products on the market rather than by the injured persons who are powerless to protect themselves." This liability is imposed with respect to all dangers, but especially concealed dangers such as defects in durability and strength of materials, dangers located in places not expected, the absence of safety features, and the absence of warnings or directions.

The rule used in torts for strict liability of sellers has been stated in the Restatement of Torts, 2nd, Section 402A as follows:

(1) One who sells any product in a defective condition unreasonably dangerous to the user or consumer or to his property is subject to liability for physical harm thereby caused to the ultimate user or consumer, or to his property, if

    (a) the seller is engaged in the business or selling such a product, and

    (b) it is expected to and does reach the user or consumer without substantial change in the condition in which it is sold.

Later cases have developed this concept to the point that proof of unreasonable danger is no longer necessary for recovery in strict tort. This whole area of product liability law is rapidly evolving, so a more in depth description of the area would not serve a helpful purpose at this time.

While most of the discussion above was directed toward the liability of manufacturers, recall that one of their duties was to provide adequate instructions and warnings. This feature of strict tort becomes important to physical educators and coaches. As experts or professionals in the field, teachers and coaches are expected to be knowledgeable about rules, techniques, safety requirements, and the equipment that they use in their occupation (see earlier chapter on instruction and coaching). Consequently, the failure of physical educators, coaches and other sport professionals to follow instructions and warnings provided by manufacturers and sellers, or the failure to teach their students and athletes these instructions and warnings, will impose strict tort liability on the teacher or coach instead of the manufacturer or seller. Once again, to avoid the imposition of strict tort, teachers and coaches must give the instructions and warnings that are provided by the producer of equipment. If these professionals do not perform this duty, there is the possibility that the administrators may also be held liable for negligence in their duty to supervise their employees. If manufacturers become aware of problems with equipment that was sold some time ago and issue new warnings or instructions, schools and institutions who are using the equipment in their programs are also subject to potential liability. Such schools may be considered as suppliers and in this situation suppliers, rather than the producer, have the duty to warn the user of the hazard. Coaches and teachers must stay current with regard to the equipment that they use during the performance of their jobs.

To summarize the above, suppliers and producers of athletic equipment may be held liable under strict tort for any product which is held to be unreasonably dangerous because of a defective condition. Such a condition will exist if the product is not reasonably fit for the ordinary purposes for which it is used and sold. The seller may avoid liability by providing proper instructions and warnings which, if followed, make the product safe. Once this condition is satisfied, the liability for injuries from the product when the instructions and warnings are not followed is placed on the provider. Coaches, teachers and program administrators may thus be found liable under strict tort.

Perhaps the equipment that best illustrates this problem in athletics is the modern football helmet. Manufacturers have worked for many years to make the helmet as safe as possible and to protect the head from injury. They have been highly successful, some argue too successful. Players began to use the helmet as a battering ram to spear opposing players or to gain a few extra yards on a run. Such activities produced neck and spinal cord injuries that left many athletes paralyzed. Many producers of helmets were found liable under strict tort and forced to give huge amounts of money to the injured youths. (See Rawlings Sporting Goods Company v. Daniels, No. 6257, Civil Court of Appeals, Tenth Judicial District, Waco, Texas, 1981, as an example.) Courts held that, in the

> # WARNING
> Do not strike an opponent with any part of this helmet or face mask. This is a violation of football rules and may cause you to suffer severe brain or neck injury including paralysis or death
> Severe brain or neck injury may also occur accidentally while playing football. NO HELMET CAN PREVENT ALL SUCH INJURIES. YOU USE THIS HELMET AT YOUR OWN RISK.

case of football helmets, a product which does not include a warning is dangerously defective. This requirement was imposed, according to the courts, because the manufacturer has greater knowledge of potential hazards than the participant. These warnings, as shown in this paragraph box, have been added to the product along with instructions for use. Changes in the rules governing the play of football were also made to take away some of the danger surrounding the use of the football helmet for purposes other than the protection of the player's head.

The logical extension of this situation occurred in 1980 when a player became quadriplegic from cervical injuries suffered during a football game. The manufacturer was, of course, sued for the negligent manufacture of the helmet and failure to warn of the limitations in its protective capabilities. This time the defendant, Rawlings Sporting Goods, interpleaded (brought in as third party defendants) the National Federation and Michigan High School Athletic Associations seeking indemnification for their negligent specifications provided for football helmets, and the principal and coaches and athletic league in which the injured party's school participated for failure to instruct and warn regarding the dangers of football helmets. (See Michael Schmidt v. Rawlings Sales Co., Inc., et al v. National Federation of State High School Associations, Inc., Michigan High School Athletic Association, Inc., et al. C.A. No. 82-73874, USDC. ED Michigan, SD.) As this development illustrates, coaches, teachers and administrators must be concerned about product liability when they fail to give warnings and instructions appropriate to the equipment that their students and athletes are using.

Warranties. A warranty is a guarantee about the integrity of a product and the maker's responsibility for the repairs and replacement of defective parts. Warranties fall into two basic categories, express and implied. Express warranties are those expressly provided, either written or verbal, with the product. Implied warranty has developed through statutory law and is codified in the Uniform Commercial Code (UCC). Two types of implied warranty are contained in the UCC; namely, the warranty of merchantability and the warranty of fitness for a particular purpose.

Section 2-314 of the UCC makes it clear that the goods delivered under an agreement must be of a quality comparable to that generally acceptable in that line of trade for goods so described and designated. This is called the warranty of merchantability. The implied warranty of fitness for a particular purpose is set forth in Section 2-315. According to its provisions, whenever a seller has reason to know at the time of the sale of the particular purpose for which the goods are required, and also that the buyer is relying on the seller's skill or judgement to select or furnish suitable goods, there is an implied warranty that the goods provided shall be fit for such purpose. Both of these provisions were adopted to give protection to consumers who did not get the goods that they bargained for, and who were confronted with disclaimers at that time by the seller when they received the substitute goods.

In addition to providing protection to the buyer and enabling him to return goods that were other than specified, these sections combined with other sections of the UCC impose liability on sellers for injuries resulting from their defective goods. Unless the institution or school becomes a seller, these sections of the UCC are of greater interest to attorneys. Just remember that the UCC provides for the return of goods that are not fit for the purpose intended when the seller knows of that purpose and knows that you are relying on his judgement. Thus, administrators should use this aspect of the code and provide adequate specifications and summaries of the intended uses of the items when requesting bids from suppliers.

SUMMARY

This chapter described the aspects of negligence related to the selection and use of athletic or other equipment. Liability may fall on the manufacturers, sellers, lessors, or other providers of equipment such as the schools if they are negligent in the production, supply, or use of the equipment, and their negligence produces injury. The three legal theories imposing liability on producers and suppliers of equipment are negligence, strict tort, and warranty. Coaches, teachers and administrators may also become liable for injuries produced by athletic equipment, if they are negligent in the performance of their duties related to that equipment. Typically, their negligence results from the use and selection of inappropriate equipment, failure to inspect the equipment for breakage or defects before use, and the failure to give adequate instructions and warnings appropriate to the equipment. Professionals must keep up to date with their knowledge and understanding of new equipment, as well as changes relative to equipment that they already have and use.

CHAPTER 6

SPORT MEDICINE

While the practice of medicine has been around for many years, the area of sport medicine and related professions is relatively new. Consequently, as is true for any rapidly developing field, the legal issues are also being developed. The status and duties of a physician, or a practitioner in a limited aspect of medicine such as a chiropractor, are rather well defined. However, until recently athletic trainers were only present in professional, college, or university sports. With the growth of sports participation and the knowledge about training, conditioning and injuries, however, athletic trainers are now engaged at all sports participation levels. In some cases the high school coach serves a dual role as athletic trainer and coach. Sport medicine also applies to those professionals who manage the "wellness" clinics or centers and cardiac rehabilitation centers, who often use physical activity in conjunction with a medical purpose. At this time it is difficult to locate case law relating to athletic training and other sport medicine personnel, so the information here will be based on the principles that generally apply to such responsibilities.

Recall that the overall duty which is imposed on all people is that they must use due care to prevent an unreasonable risk of injury to others. Thus, the school, club, or institution must take other actions necessary to meet this duty. In the case of injuries to participants or others, the duty becomes one of preventing further injury or harm to that party. To accomplish this task, the administrator should make sure that a survey of the facilities and programs was performed to determine what types of injuries are probable, and then to purchase the first-aid and emergency equipment needed to meet these situations. For example, an aquatics program should have a back-board present to remove people with back injuries from the water safely; football programs should have splints available, and so on.

The second step is that all personnel should be trained in first aid and appropriate emergency procedures. Coaches have been found liable for their failure to have and use adequate first aid training (Mogabgab v. Orleans Parish School Board). Coaches should have special knowledge about the particular types of problems that they may face. Football coaches, in particular, should know the signs and procedures relating to heat disorders, for example. Non-medical personnel should not attempt to perform more than first aid. If they should attempt a procedure that is classified as medical, they will likely be held to the standard of care used for physicians (Butler v. Louisiana State Board of Education, 331 S. 2d 192, LA app. 1976). Here a biology professor who supervised a project involving the taking of blood samples was held to the level of care imposed on physicians. State laws usually describe what may be considered as the practice of medicine or other professions, and so one should not perform tasks specifically designated as medical by statute.

To summarize, the persons and organizations in charge of the sports activity have two duties with regard to injuries suffered in connection with that activity. First, they have a duty to provide or secure reasonable medical assistance for the injured party, either participant or spectator, as soon as possible under the circumstances. Second, if such medical assistance is not immediately available, the duty of care will require that the injured party be transported to a place where medical care can be provided as soon as is reasonably possible. The added requirement that the injured party be properly cared for until medical assistance can be rendered is also imposed (Clark v. State; Mogabgab v. Orleans Parish School Board). Thus, proper first aid, proper handling, and the necessary first-aid equipment must be provided to meet these duties. At least one court has defined reasonable medical assistance as the provision of reasonable facilities and equipment, as well as persons with the necessary degree of skill and experience (Clark v. State). If the persons in charge perform unnecessary or detrimental acts, they will, in all probability, find themselves liable for any harm that resulted.

ATHLETIC TRAINERS

According to a career publication brochure of the National Athletic Trainers Association (NATA), the trainer's duties consist of implementing prevention of injury programs and immediate treatment and rehabilitation procedures for the injured athlete as directed by the team physician ("Athletic Training: Careers, Placement," 1984). An athletic trainer is defined by the NATA as a person who has met the athletic training curriculum requirements of an accredited college or university and who, upon the advice and consent of his team and/or consulting physician, carries out the practice of prevention and/or physical rehabilitation of injuries incurred by athletes. To carry out these functions, the athletic trainer is authorized to utilize modalities such as heat, light, sound, cold, electricity, or mechanical devices related to rehabilitation and treatment ("Guidelines for the Implementation of Legislation for State Licensure of Athletic Trainers," Sections 2 & 10, National Athletic Trainers Association). The status of athletic trainers can vary considerably from state to state, as the statutory regulations may either be present in a differing form or be non-existent. Consequently, the trainer should make sure what types of tasks can legally be done and what may be prohibited.

In a recent publication (NATA, 1992), the Professional Education Committee provided a job description categorized into six major domains which make up the role of the Certified Athletic Trainer: Prevention, Recognition and Evaluation, Management/Treatment and Disposition, Rehabilitation, Organization and Administration, and Education and Counseling. Each of these domains is, in turn, composed of several competencies. This publication provides considerably more detail than the earlier Guidelines described above. The structure of program accreditation in athletic training has also recently changed. The Committee on Allied Health Education and Accreditation (CAHEA) now grants accreditation to academic programs preparing athletic trainers rather than the NATA.

A further important change in athletic training is in the way professional certified trainers are supervised. States are now including athletic training with occupational therapy and physical therapy, which means the practice of athletic training is therefore controlled by the Occupational Therapy, Physical Therapy and Athletic Training Board. As an example, see the Ohio Revised Code Section 4755.60, *et seq.*, which defines athletic training, practice, ethical behavior, creates licensure, and sets qualifications for athletic trainers. Athletic trainers must now be aware of legislative changes impacting on their profession.

As indicated above, one part of the athletic trainer's job is that of preparation for athletic contests. Several different tasks have been assigned to athletic trainers relating to this part of his job. The trainer may be involved in screening tasks such as evaluating flexibility, strength and other abilities related to safe participation in sports. The trainer may be responsible for receiving and evaluating the medical screening forms provided by physicians. In some institutions the athletic trainer is responsible for developing the physical conditioning program used to develop physical fitness. While involved with sports that take place in high temperature and high humidity conditions, the trainer should determine if practice must be modified. During such environmental conditions, the trainer has the responsibility to supervise the pre- and post-practice weighing of players to make sure that they have not lost too much water and to supervise their water intake during practice. The same duty applies to the athletic trainer while performing these duties as for instructors and coaches during teaching and coaching; he or she must exercise due care to avoid subjecting others to an unreasonable risk of injury (see Chapter 2, Negligence).

If an athlete should have an injury, the athletic trainer is expected to determine if medical assistance is required and, if so, to make sure that the athlete receives such medical aid. After the injury has been treated by the physician, the trainer is expected to supervise the rehabilitation program and to perform taping or other supportive assistance as necessary. The rehabilitation may involve the use of exercise and physical activity, or it may involve the use of such modalities as cold and heat. In the case of injuries, the athletic trainer is subject to the same duties as other persons administering athletic programs. All have a duty to provide or secure reasonable medical assistance for the injured party as soon as possible under the circumstances. If such medical assistance is not immediately available, the duty of care will require that the injured party be transported to a place where medical care can be provided as soon as is reasonably possible. As described above, if the athletic trainer should attempt an act that falls outside of the job and is part of another profession, the trainer will be judged by the standard of care that is applied to that profession.

> POTENTIAL PROBLEM AREA: Insurance coverage of players' injuries if their primary coverage is through an HMO and approval is required before treatment.

A search of the case law surrounding the liability of athletic trainers disclosed little pertinent common law as most case law situations involved either coaches and/or physicians. This situation probably exists because in most high school situations the coach also serves as an athletic trainer. There have been several state and national attempts to legislate that athletic trainers are required to be present at sporting events. If such laws should develop, and athletic trainers become more visible and plentiful, case law relating to such a profession will probably also develop. In the interim, the best practice is to have adequate training in first-aid and athletic training procedures, to perform only those acts that are within the scope of athletic training, and to exercise due care to prevent injuries from happening. When they do happen, exercise due care so that the injury is not made worse.

One example of the legal issues faced by athletic trainers is provided by the following case ("Jury Clears . . . ," 1989). A Kent State University athletic trainer was tried on allegations that someone other than a physician was writing and filling orders for prescription drugs. Ohio Revised Code stipulated that only physicians can write prescriptions and only physicians or pharmacists can dispense prescription medication. During the trial, testimony indicated that the trainer never held himself out to be a doctor or received compensation from the athletes. All medication was given to athletes after consultation with a doctor. A member of the Ohio State Board of Pharmacy defined dispensing as "putting a prescription drug in a container, labeling it, and handing it to a patient." Thus, the case hinged on a technical interpretation of law. The jury decided that the trainer was not guilty of violating the Ohio Revised Code. The trainer can evaluate and rehabilitate and a doctor can delegate authority to an athletic trainer to dispense medicine. This case serves to illustrate the need for sound administration and organizational procedures as well as the need to document activities carried out in the training room.

In Gillespie v. Southern Utah State College, an injured student athlete sought to recover for negligence and injuries allegedly caused by tight taping of his sprained ankle and ice immersion treatments. The athlete suffered a disability after amputation of a gangrenous toe and removal of muscle and tissue on his right foot. The plaintiff received verbal instructions as to the care of his injury, but he apparently slept through the night with his ankle submerged in a bucket of ice water. The jury found for the trainer and university. However, the lesson to be learned from this case is that trainers must make sure the athletes they treat understand what is expected from them. One way to show that the trainer gave clear directions is to provide the athlete with written directions, with a copy placed in his or her file, explaining what to do and not to do.

Athletic trainers must also pay attention to record-keeping. All medical records are confidential and should not be released without the athlete's permission. Likewise, federal law makes all academic and personal files confidential and subject to the same requirements. If the athlete wishes that his or her medical records be sent to a professional team or another person, the athlete should sign a release for those records and be informed that, once those records are released, the school has no control over the manner in which the other party will use the records. The athlete must be made aware that his or her cause may be either helped or hurt by the release of the records. Make sure that an accident form is completed for all injuries describing the type and extent of injury, how it occurred, and what action was taken for the injury. These forms should be also completed when any staff are injured for use in case of workman's compensation claims. Record-keeping is important to show how the prevention and rehabilitation aspects of the job are completed.

PHYSICIANS

Extensive case law has evolved about the legal duties which apply to physicians. These duties include the following: (1) to act with utmost good faith toward the patients; (2) to advise the patient about the effectiveness of the treatment being considered; (3) to refer the patient to a more successful treatment if such a treatment exists; (4) to perform a proper diagnosis; (5) to exercise due care during the treatment of the patient; and (6) to insure continuity of treatment for his patients (King, 1977). Several of these duties require the assistance of the coach, athletic trainer or other officials. For example, the physician's first duty is to the adequate care of the patient, not to the team or school. He should not return the player to participation until the player can be declared medically able to participate. Dick Butkus received a large out-of-court settlement because the team physician was also a part-owner of the team which he played for as a professional. According to Mr. Butkus, he was returned to action before his knees were "medically ready," and this subsequently limited his playing career. Consequently, if the physician does not permit participation, coaches must accept that situation and act accordingly. To provide continuity of treatment, the coach or trainer may have to supervise the athletes to make sure they comply with the doctor's directions. In many high schools, volunteer physicians serve as team doctors at the game. If any injury occurs, and the doctor requests that the injured player see his personal physician the next day, the coach or trainer should make sure that the player follows through with this direction. The follow-up visit is necessary for continuity, and also because the coach may be found negligent if he lets the player practice when he knows that the player should have been examined further.

> Physicians must act in the best interest of the athlete, not the team.

Several approaches have been used to determine the standard of care expected of physicians. The most frequently used standard of care is that the physician is under a duty to employ those practices that a reasonably competent member of the profession practicing in the same specialty would be expected to do in order to conform to the approved professional practice. In the case of practitioners in either the specialties or allied health care fields, the courts have generally held such individuals to the professional standards of other similarly situated members of the specialty or field in which they practice (King, 1977).

In the legal system, the concept of medical malpractice has evolved to represent the system of loss allocation that is based, for the most part, on the fault of the defendant physician.

42

Malpractice results from conduct below the level that society allows with impunity, rather than the mere fact that a patient has suffered a health-impairing experience during the course of a medical procedure. Generally, whenever a physician undertakes to render care to a person, a professional relationship between the physician and that person is established, and a corresponding duty of care to the patient is created as described above. For the most part, any liability that arises from this relationship is a problem for the physician rather than the schools. However, exceptions do arise.

As an example, in Welch v. Dunsmuir Joint Union High School District, a high school quarterback sustained an injury following which he was unable to get to his feet. When his coach arrived, the injured athlete was able to move his hands at his coach's direction. He was then carried to the sidelines by teammates with no supervision given to the manner in which he was transported. When he arrived at the sidelines, he was unable to move either his hands or his feet. Although a physician was in attendance during this period of time, it is not clear whether he examined the player on the field or only at the sidelines. In any event, the boy was rendered a permanent quadriplegic through these events and brought suit against the school, the coach, and the doctor. Testimony during the trial established that the spinal cord was not severed at the time of injury, since he could move his hands. Thus, the severance could only have occurred when he was being carried from the field. The jury issued a verdict against all defendants. The negligence of the doctor was apparently his failure to treat the athlete immediately on the field, and to instruct the others as to how he should be carried from the field. The school officials did not follow appropriate transport and first-aid procedures and were liable for this negligence.

The point is that athletic administrators should develop procedures that will minimize the potential for situations like that described above to develop. Some suggestions that should be implemented are as follows:

1. Regardless of the status of your team physician, volunteer or paid, complete a written contract or agreement so all parties understand the responsibilities of each other.

2. Determine what equipment the school is responsible for providing, and what equipment will be supplied by the physician.

3. Establish procedures for the appropriate transfer of persons needing medical attention beyond the capabilities present in your school situation.

4. Develop job descriptions for all personnel associated with athletic and physical education programs: coaches, teachers, nurses, athletic trainers and physicians.

5. Keep records! Fill out accident reports, keep training and medical records, document your "follow-up" procedures. The physician who renders emergency care should not be required to attend the patient once he or she has been referred to the patient's family physician or hospital emergency personnel and that fact has been communicated to the patient. If your player or student is to see the family physician before returning to practice or class, make sure that he or she did so. Usually the relationship between the team physician and the injured athlete is not a permanent one, and the coach may be negligent if the coach does not follow up to make sure his athlete's behavior complies with directions.

6. Make sure that the proper screening occurred with the pre-season physical examination. In some states, only doctors of medicine or osteopathy can certify fitness for participation. The objective of the medical examination should be to discover problems in

impaired organs, occult sites, mental and physical retardation, and seemingly innocuous defects or other abnormalities that may present problems. School personnel should inspect the completed medical examination form to make sure that all requirements were met ("What You Don't Know Can Hurt You," Proceedings of the Law and Sports Conference). Chiropractors and other practitioners of "limited" medical professions often desire to sign the medical approval forms. They can sign and grant limited approval only for those tests they can legally perform. Before accepting such approval, make sure that all the required aspects of the examination have been completed. Do not accept partially completed medical examinations as complete approval for participation. If someone should insist that you do so, either get an opinion from your state's attorney general (and keep it on file) or refuse and let them bring suit so the courts can settle the issue.

ATHLETES WITH MEDICAL CONDITIONS

With the emphasis that sports and athletic participation has today, many youths desire to participate in athletic programs. Unfortunately, some youths may have conditions, such as the loss of sight in one eye or only one functioning kidney, that make their participation in some activities more dangerous than it is for a person having complete function in all organs. Further, the screening examination may detect some congenital conditions that also increase the risk to that person. Under such circumstances, many physicians refuse to give medical permission for participation. A number of these cases have resulted in suits to make the school allow the student to participate. In most situations, the courts have refused to order the schools to let the student participate. The resulting legal principles can vary from area to area, so this is an issue that you as a coach or administrator should watch closely. In at least one case, a star performer was involved; so be careful to avoid a conflict of interest. Remember that the physician's duty is to act in the best interest of his patient, not the team. Parents will often offer to sign releases or waivers if the school will permit the student to participate. This offer may appear tempting, but remember that courts have consistently held that parents cannot sign away the right of their child to sue for injuries caused through negligent acts, even if a waiver has been signed. This entire situation could result in expensive and devastating consequences. Use good judgement and be conservative; more is at stake than winning or losing an athletic contest or two.

Legislation, such as the Americans with Disabilities Act and the Rehabilitation Act of 1973, has resulted in increased participation opportunities for handicapped individuals. For example, one result of this legislation has been that individuals who have been exposed to and/or tested positive for the HIV or HTLV-III or LAV virus, must be allowed to attend regular school classes and participate in any of the wide variety of programs for which they are qualified. The common name for the condition resulting from this virus is Acquired Immune Deficiency Syndrome (AIDS) or AIDS-related complex (ARC). Three issues come to mind: (1) the duty possessed by the HIV positive individual to prevent unreasonable risk of harm to others from exposure to his or her disease; (2) the duty of the schools and school personnel to prevent unreasonable risk of injury to students in their care; and (3) the duty of physicians to warn third parties about "a serious threat of danger" from patients they are treating (Drowatzky, 1988). Legal answers to these and other questions have not been definitively given.

Earlier, the point was made that participants assume the inherent risks present in the activities in which they participate. Thus, the question arises, does possible exposure to the HIV virus constitute an inherent risk of participation? If so, should the athletes be told of specific participants who are HIV positive or just that such risk might be present? A focus on these issues was provided through the announcement by Ervin "Magic" Johnson of his HIV positive status and participation in the Olympic Games. Does the fact that he is a professional athlete change the assumption of the risk defense? Currently, the Public Health Services Act requires notification to emergency response employees about individuals with AIDS or HIV, HTLV-III or LAV positive test results so they can distinguish between conditions in which such employees are at risk. Logically, athletic trainers, school nurses and other school-employed emergency response personnel should be informed of the presence of individuals having those conditions (Drowatzky, 1989a). In the absence of other policies, the schools must formulate prevention procedures, not only for AIDS or HIV positive individuals, but also for exposure to those having hepatitis and other communicable diseases. This is an area currently undergoing changes and administrators must keep up to date with new policies (Drowatzky, 1989b; Herbert, 1989).

These changes place increased emphasis on the statement that "athletic trainers must keep current with their education." Not only must trainers know the characteristics of "normal" athletes, but they must also understand limitations and special needs of athletes having handicapping conditions. Placing athletic trainers under control of state professional boards has both positive and negative impact on the practice of athletic trainers. Professionals must know the limitations and requirements imposed by state boards of practice.

SUMMARY

The whole area of sport medicine is rapidly developing. In the past few years, physicians have begun to specialize in sports injuries, and more teams are now using athletic trainers. The area of sport medicine therefore involves people from many and varied professions: coaches, athletic trainers, physical therapists, and physicians, for example. So long as professionals stay within the accepted practices of their field, they will be held to the standard of care requiring the use of the skills and techniques commonly used by members of their profession. However, as soon as a person practices activities commonly performed by another profession, he or she will be held to the standard of care applied to that profession.

Persons in charge of sports activities have a duty to provide or secure reasonable medical assistance for injured persons as soon as possible under the circumstances. If the necessary medical aid is not readily available, the injured party must be properly cared for until medical assistance can be rendered. Courts commonly require the availability of reasonable facilities and equipment, the application of first aid, and proper handling in order to meet the duty of reasonable medical assistance. It makes no difference whether the injured party is participant, spectator, or visitor. In view of the duty to use reasonable care imposed on all parties, the duty to provide reasonable medical assistance, and the variety of professions involved, the administrator must make sure that proper coordination among those persons involved in sport medicine is present. Finally, because sport medicine is a developing area, the legal duties and issues related to sport medicine are also developing. Consequently, it is important to keep up with the continuing education provided for those in the field.

REFERENCES

American Law Institute. *Restatement of agency, second: Agency 2d.* St. Paul, MN: American Law Institute Publishers, 1958.

American Law Institute. *Restatement of torts, second: Torts 2d.* St. Paul, MN: American Law Institute Publishers, 1965.

American Law Reports (ALR3d). Volume 38. Rochester, N.Y.: The Lawyers Cooperative Publishing Co., 1970.

Armlin v. Board of Education, 320 N.Y.S. 2d 402 (1971).

"Athletic Training: Careers, Placement." National Athletic Trainers Association, Inc., Information Brochure, 1984.

Bally v. Northeastern University, 532 N.E.2d 49 (Mass. 1989).

Banfield v. Louis, 589 So. 2d 441 (1991).

Bauer v. Board of Education of the City of New York, 140 N.Y.S. 2d 167 (N.Y. 1953).

Bearman v. University of Notre Dame, 453 N.E. 2d 1196 (Ind. 1983).

Behagen v. Intercollegiate Conference of Faculty Representatives, 346 F. Supp. 602 (D. Minn. 1972).

Bellman v. San Francisco High School District, 81 P. 2d 984 (1938).

Benjamin v. State, 453 N.Y.S. 2d 329 (N.Y. 1982).

Bourque v. Duplechin, 331 So. 2d 40 (L.A. App. 1976).

Bragg v. Central New England R. Co., 126 N.E. 253 (1920).

Brahatcek v. Millard School District, School District #17, 273 N.W. 2d 680 (Neb. 1979).

Brown v. Wichita State University, 540 P.2d 66, 217 Kan 279, vac in part on other grounds 547 P.2d 1015, 219 Kan 2, app. dismissed 97 S.Ct. 41, 429 US 806, 50 L.Ed. 2d 67.

Buchan v. U.S. Cycling Federation, Inc., 227 Cal. Rptr. 887 (1991).

Bugger v. Iowa High School Association, 197 N.W. 2d 555 (Iowa 1972).

Calmari, J.D. and Perillo, J.M. *The law of contracts.* St. Paul, MN: West, 1970.

Carabba v. Anacortes School District #103, 435 P. 2d 936 (Wash. 1967).

Certificate of Employment, The University of Toledo. Toledo, OH: 1992.

Cherney v. Board of Education of the City School District of White Plains, 297 N.Y.S. 2d 668 (N.Y. 1969).

Chester v. World Football League, 255 N.W. 2d 643.

Chicago Terminal Transfer R. Co. v. Kotoski, 65 N.E. 350 (1902).

Chilton v. Cook County School District No. 207, Maine Township, 325 N.E. 2d 666 (Ill. 1975).

Cirillo v. City of Milwaukee, 150 N.W. 2d 460 (Wisc. 1967).

Clark v. State, 99 N.E. 2d 309 (1951).

Darrow v. West Genesee Central School District, 41 A.D. 2d 987, 342 N.Y.S. 2d 611 (1963).

Davis, K. C. *Administrative law text.* (3rd ed.). St. Paul, MN: West, 1972.

Diker v. City of St. Louis Park, 130 N.W. 2d 133 (1964).

Doyle v. Bowdoin College v. Cooper International, 403 A. 2d 1206 (MA: 1979).

Drowatzky, J. N. On the firing line: negligence in physical education. *Journal of Law and Education,* 6, 481–490 (1977).

Drowatzky, John N. AIDS Victims' Participation in Sports. *Sports, Parks & Recreation Law Reporter,* 2, (1), 1, 5–6 (June 1988).

Drowatzky, John N. Implications of AIDS in Sports: The Need for Policies and Procedures. *Sports, Parks & Recreation Law Reporter,* 3, (3), 41, 43-46 (December, 1989b).

Drowatzky, John N. Tort Law, AIDS and Participation in Sports. *Sports, Parks & Recreation Law Reporter,* 2, (4), 56–59 (March, 1989a).

Dunham v. Pulsifer, 312 F. Supp. 411 (D. Vt. 1970).

Eddy v. Syracuse University, 433 N.Y.S. 2d 923 (App. Div. 1980).

Fein v. Board of Education of New York, 111 N.E. 2d 732 (1953).

Gardner v. State, 22 N.E. 2d 344 (N.Y. 1938).

Gillespie v. Southern Utah State College, 669 P. 2d 861 (Utah, 1983).

Goss v. Lopez, 419 U.S. 565 (1975).

Grant v. Lake Oswego School District No. 7, Clackamas County, 515 P. 2d 947 (Ore. 1974).

Greenman v. Yuba Power Products, Inc., 377 P. 2d 897 (1962).

Hackbart v. Cincinnati Bengals, Inc. and Charles "Booby" Clark, 435 F.Supp. 352 (D.Colo. 1977), reversed 601 F.2d 516 (10th Cir. 1979), certiorari denied 100 S.Ct 275, 444 U.S. 931, 62 L.Ed.2d 188 (1979).

Hanna v. State, 258 N.Y.S. 2d 694 (1965).

Hazard, William R. *Education and the law.* (2nd ed.). New York: Free Press, 1978.

Herbert, David L. The Development of AIDS Guidelines for Sports Programs. *Sports, Parks & Recreation Law Reporter,* 3, (1), 12-18 June 1989.

Hill v. NCAA, 273 Cal Rptr. 402 (Cal. App. 6 Dist 1990).

"Jury Clears Kent State ATC on Charges of 'Practicing Medicine.'" *NATA News: Newsletter of The National Athletic Trainers' Association,* 2, 1, 1, 7 & 15 (Fall, 1989).

Keesee v. Board of Education of the City of New York, 235 N.Y.S. 2d 300 (N.Y. 1962).

Kelly v. Board of Education of the City of New York, 180 N.Y.S. 2d 130 (Ct. 1920).

Kelly v. Metropolitan County School Board, 293 F. Supp. 485 (M.D. Tenn. 1968).

Kerby v. Elk Grove Union High School District, 36 P. 2d 431 (1934).

King. H. *The Law of Medical Malpractice.* St. Paul, MN: West, 1977.

Lamphear v. State, 458 N.Y.S. 2d 71 (App. Div. 1982).

Langerman, S. and Fidel, N. Responsibility is also part of the game. *Trial,* 13 (1977), 22-25.

Latty, E.R. and Frampton, G.T. Basic business associations. In H. M. Friedman (Ed.), *Materials on the law of agency.* Toledo, OH: The University of Toledo, 1977.

Macek v. Schooner's Inc., 586 N.E. 2d 442 (1991).

Mogabgab v. Orleans Parish School Board, 239 S. 2d 456 (La. App. 1970).

Monfils v. City of Sterling Heights, 269 N.W. 2d 258 (1978).

NATA, Professional Educational Committee. *Competencies in Athletic Training.* Dallas: National Athletic Trainers' Association, 1992.

Nabozny v. Barnhill, 334 N.E. 2d 258 (Ill. 1975).

Noel, D.W. and Phillips, J.J. *Products liability.* (2nd ed.). St. Paul, MN: West, 1981.

O'Halloran v. University of Washington, 679 F.Supp. 997 (W.D.Wash, 1988); (revd on other grounds (9th Cir.) 856 F. 2d 1375).

1 Wiliston, *Contracts,* Section 1 (3rd. ed.)., 1907.

Proehl, P.O. Liability of teachers. *Vanderbilt Law Review,* 12 (1959), 723–756.

Prosser, W.L. *Handbook of the law of torts.* (4th ed.). St. Paul, MN: West, 1971.

Rivera v. Board of Education of City of New York, 201 N.Y.S. 2d 372 (1960).

Russo v. Texas & Pac. R. Co., 181 So. 485 (1938).

Sales, J.B. The duty to warn and instruct for safe use in strict tort liability. *St. Mary's Law Journal,* (1982), 521.

Scaduto v. State, 446 N.Y.S. 2d 529 (N.Y. 1982).

Short v. Griffitts, 255 S.E. 2d 479 (1979).

Terry, H.T. Negligence. *Harvard Law Review,* 29 (1915), 40.

Tymkowicz v. San Jose Unified School District, 312 P. 2d 388 (Cal. 1957).

Tyson v. Eastern Carolina R. Co., 83 S.E. 318 (1914).

Uniform commercial code. Philadelphia, PA: The American Law Institute, 1980.

Vacca, R.S. Teacher malpractice. *University of Richmond Law Review,* 8, 447–457 (1974).

Vendrell v. School District No. 26C, 376 P. 2d 406 (1962).

Welch v. Dunsmuir Joint Union High School District, 326 P. 2d 633 (Cal. App. 1958).

What you don't know can hurt you. *Proceedings of the Law and Sports Conference.* Winston-Salem, N.C.: Sports and the Courts, 1983.

Wilkinson v. Hartford Accident and Indemnity Company, 411 So. 2d 22 (La. 1982).

Williams v. Cox Enterprises, Inc., 283 S.E. 2d 367 (1981).

Woodring v. Board of Education of Manhasset Union Free School District, 435 N.Y.S. 2d 52 (1981).

Yazoo and M.V.R. Co. v. Lee, 114 So. 866 (1927).

ABOUT THE AUTHOR

Name:
John N. Drowatzky

Birth Place:
Wichita, Kansas U.S.A.

Formal Education:
B.S., University of Kansas
M.S., University of Oregon
Ed.D., University of Oregon
J.D., The University of Toledo

Present Position:
Professor of Exercise Science and Physical Education, The University of Toledo, Toledo, Ohio 43606

Professional Responsibilities:
Teaching undergraduate and graduate students the areas of Motor Learning, Sport Law, Adapted Physical Education and Corrective Therapy

Scholarly Interests:
Writing and research has focused on the areas of motor learning and law of sport.

Professional Accomplishments:
Books written include (Editor) *Abstracts of Research Papers, 1970: AAHPER Convention; Physical Education for the Mentally Retarded,* Lea & Febiger, 1971, Translated into Spanish by Editorial Medica, Pan Americana, Buenos Aires, 1973; *Motor Learning: Principles and Practices,* Burgess, 1975, 2nd ed., 1981; *Physical Education: Career Perspectives and Professional Foundations* (w/C. Armstrong). Prentice-Hall, 1984, 2nd ed., 1992. Published more than 50 articles in various professional journals. Professional affiliations include AAHPERD; Fellow, Research Consortium; Fellow, American Academy of Physical Education, Phi Epsilon Kappa, Phi Delta Kappa; Society for the Study of Legal Aspects of Sport and Physical Activity; Admitted to practice before the Ohio Bar; Expert Witness in Sport Injury Cases.

Hobbies:
Fishing, swimming, tennis, reading, photography, and travel.

Honors & Awards:
Faculty Research Fellowship sponsored by the Graduate School of The University of Toledo, 1968; Certificate of Recognition by the Lucas County Association for Mentally Retarded Persons, 1970; Hope Anchor Plaque for Service at Hope Lutheran Church, 1974; Adjunct Professor of Psychology and Physical Education at the University of Oregon, 1976; Corpus Juris Secundum Award for Significant Legal Scholarship, 1978; Certificate of Attestation, University of Londrina, Brazil, 1981; Who's Who in the Midwest, 1980; International Who's Who of Contemporary Achievement, 1981; Men of Achievement, 1981; Personalities of America, 1982; Community Leaders of the World, 1982; Two Thousand Notable Americans, 1984; International Book of Honor, 1984. Carl Haven Young Service Award for Meritorious Service presented by the American Kinesiotherapy Association, 1986; Certificate of Recognition for Contributions to Mentally Retarded Individuals by the Northwest Ohio Development Center, Ohio Department of Mental Retardation and Developmental Disabilities, 1987.